CW00338527

Upper Nithsdale Folklore

compiled and edited by
Rog Wood

Illustrated by
Gary Bonn

First published 2011

© Copyright Rog Wood

The right of Rog Wood to be identified as the author of this work has been asserted by
him in accordance with the Copyright, Designs and Patents Act, 1988.

All rights reserved. No part of this work may be reproduced,
stored in a retrieval system, or transmitted, in any form or by any means,
electronic, mechanical, optical, photocopying, recording or otherwise,
without the written permission of Rog Wood.

Design, set and print by
Solway Offset *the* Printers, Dumfries
for the publisher, Creedon Publications

ISBN 978-1-907931-03-01

Creedon Publications, 11 Catherinefield Industrial Estate, Heathhall, Dumfries

Foreword

This is Rog Wood's second venture into the folklore of Nithsdale. His first was *Old Sanquhar Tales*, which breathed new life into stories that had not been told for a century and more. Rog's wide experience as a journalist and author enabled him to present them to a modern readership, and his local farming background kept them rooted in the land of his birth. The result was – success! The *Tales* has proved popular with locals and expatriates alike, and sales have been strong.

Upper Nithsdale Folklore is destined to repeat, if not surpass, the popularity of the first book. The scope is broader, taking in all the parishes from Morton and Tynron to Kirkconnel, and the depth and variety of the content is greater. Ghosts, fairies and Covenanters appear again, but so do a host of other Nithsdale folk. The story of "the mightiest production of Penpont parish", John McCall of Glenmanna, and his exploits is a gem. The devotees of curling, "Old Q" and Robert Burns all play their parts, and the resulting mix of story, anecdote and historical fact is enticing. Many who read *Upper Nithsdale Folklore* will find their appetite for local history whetted; they will discover that there is a vast treasury of sources to satisfy them.

Folklore is often seen as the poor relation of history, but historical "fact" is often proved false. It is sometimes through the stories people loved to tell, through the light this sheds on their own viewpoints and concerns, that a glimpse of the truth about the past can be discerned. Rog Wood has collected and re-told a selection of such stories in this book, and is to be commended for it.

Graham Roberts
Local Studies Coordinator, Ewart Library.

Rog Wood

Gary Bonn

Contents

Acknowledgements

Following on from the success of my last collection of local folklore, *Old Sanquhar Tales*, I have compiled this collection, *Upper Nithsdale Folklore*, to cover a wider geographical area that includes Cairndale, Tynron, Penpont, Thornhill, Durisdeer, Wanlockhead and Kirkoconnel as well as Sanquhar. I hope readers get as much pleasure from this collection as they told me they got from *Old Sanquhar Tales*.

I would like to thank local artist Gary Bonn for his illustrations and local photographer Stewart Readman for the cover photograph of Drumlanrig Castle. I would also like to thank local scribes Willie Dalgleish and Sheila Crompton, and Graham Roberts of the Ewart Library Service for painstakingly proof reading the draft document.

I would also like to acknowledge the following as sources of material for this book: The Trustees of the Wanlockhead Lead Mining Museum Trust; *The Martyr Graves of Scotland* by J H Thomson, *Traditions of the Covenanters, Martyrland* and *History of Sanquhar*, all three books by Robert Simpson; *Old Q* by Henry Blyth; *Drumlanrig and the Douglases* by Crawford Tait Ramage; *Thornhill and its Worthies* by J L Waugh; *The Annals of an Inland Parish, Glencairn, Dumfriesshire* by John Corrie; *The Laird of Lag* by Alexander Fergusson; *Closeburn, Reminiscent, Historic and Traditional* by R M F Watson; *James Shaw, A Country Schoolmaster* by Robert Wallace; *Memorials of Sanquhar Kirkyard* by Tom Wilson; *History of Sanquhar* by James Brown; *Annals of Sanquhar* by Tom Wilson and W McMillan; *Folk Lore and Genealogies of Uppermost Nithsdale* by William Wilson; *Burns and Black Joan* by T Wilson; *God's Treasure House of Scotland* by Rev. J Moir Porteous and finally, an address to the *Sanquhar Heritage Society* by Kenneth McLean using the *History of Sanquhar Curling Society* by James Brown as its principal source of information.

I would also like to thank Mr H Kerr and the Ewart Library for allowing me to reproduce some of their old black and white photographs.

Rog Wood

Chapter 1
The legend of Morton Castle

Morton Castle, a stronghold now in ruins, occupies a commanding position in a wild and secluded locality to the east of Thornhill. Built on a projecting brow over a narrow valley, it reared its frowning turrets in the midst of dark, surrounding woods. From the top of its massive walls, that seem to have been built "for all time", the warder could keep watch all around him as far as the eye could see. The blast of his bugle horn at the dead of night, when danger was near, sounded afar over hill and glen. That would send echoes through the forest to awake and startle the deer that slept securely in the covert and summon from their slumbering beds the faithful retainers of the old baron to aid him in his hour of peril.

The scene around the baronial seat is one of wild grandeur. The hills on the north, lofty and rugged, present immeasurable tracts of brown heath and large spaces occupied with grey rocks and scattered stones. Their wooded glens and deep ravines afforded, in times of persecuting violence, places of retreat to the Covenanters who were forced to flee to the remotest solitude to hide themselves from the fury of their oppressors. In surveying the harsher features of the scene, no one could suspect that there were spots of unsurpassed beauty concealed in the bosom of these dreary heights, or that there were places where the silvery burn meanders with willows drooping over its streams as it leaves the upland wastes to visit the distant ocean.

As deeds of darkness were perpetrated in the vicinity of these feudal halls, stories of great events have no doubt been common here as elsewhere.

There are place-names in the vicinity of the castle which show that the possessor of the barony had the right of pit and gallows. (Condemned women were drowned by tying them in a sack that was thrown into a pit full of water, while condemned men were hung from the gallows). Nearby, on the hill east of the castle stood an old thorn, that was eventually uprooted centuries ago in a storm, but which was known as the Judgement Thorn. Close to the farm-steading of Morton Mains are Gallows Flat and Hanging Shaw, where doom of judgement was carried into execution.

The gloomy scenery contributed to the fostering of a superstitious dread in the breast of the traveller who, under the cloud of night, was obliged to

Condemned women were drowned tied in a sack

pursue his way through a lonely glen, or haunted grove. When the yellow ray of the wintry moon was unable to penetrate the thick veil of clouds that overshadowed her, and when the breath of the coming storm blew aside for a moment her cloudy covering, the yellow glare that fell upon the leafless woods served only to make the scene more dismal and dreary. There was not a voice to disturb the solitary meditations of the night-time wanderer, save the howling wind and the lonely murmur of the waters, lamenting the decayed beauty of the woods and the desolation of the stormy winter.

Tradition informs us that, in the Morton Castle in medieval times, when warlike chieftains exercised the power of life and death within their own domain, there was a young man in the service of the baron. This youth was both well-mannered and handsome, and devoted to his master and faithful to his interests. He loved a girl who lived on the banks of the Carron – a pleasant stream that winds its way through the ancient parish of Durisdeer and falls into the Nith opposite the policies of Drumlanrig Castle. Its course is not lengthy, but it flows through enchanting scenery. The girl, whose name was Agnes, lived with her parents in a cottage among the woods in the valley.

She was the fairest of the daughters of Carron Valley. All who saw Agnes loved her for none was more beautiful and none more kind and considerate. Among the girls who met on the cottage green, or in the sunny glades of the flowery woods, to sing their favourite songs, none sang as charmingly as she did. Agnes was the darling of her parents.

Carronbridge about 1900

Edward, the youth of the castle, had long cherished a love for Agnes – long indeed before he mustered courage to whisper it in her ear. At length he revealed the secret and he had the satisfaction to know that its discovery was not unacceptable. From that moment they were a happy couple and only waited the proper time when they should be man and wife.

Edward's sweetest hours were spent with his Agnes and her image was never long absent from his mind. But there were others who looked lovingly on Edward besides his darling Agnes – and among these was his own mistress. This woman had long cherished a passion for her servant and one day, in the absence of her lord, she confessed her affection to him. The declaration was revolting to the mind of the generous youth. He retreated from her presence, but first told her that his heart was wholly given to the maid of Carron and that on no account would he give his love and his honour to another.

The lady of the castle was mortified at the rejection, as she felt that it was a severe censure on the baseness of her conduct. Love and fear now struggled in her breast. She loved the youth and she feared it becoming known. At length fear prevailed and in order to protect her reputation and her safety, she decided to work the ruin of the virtuous Edward. She ruminated in her solitary chamber on the best way of accomplishing this and finally decided to falsely accuse him of having made improper advances towards her. Accordingly, having decided her plan of revenge, she waited patiently on the baron's return. Edward, in the meantime, was unaware of the storm that was gathering over him.

At length the look-out on the castle walls announced the coming of the doughty chieftain with a company of his horsemen, threading their way through the woods and appearing now and then in full array in the opening glades of the thickets. It was the evening of an overcast, humid day. The sultry atmosphere had led to the sky filling with dark clouds. The dark hills and the grey turrets of the castle were surrounded by a more than usual gloom. The sheep were gathering on the hills, the birds were leaving the open sky and cowering down among the leafy branches of the woods, and the hoarse mutterings of thunder were heard far away among the distant hills.

The baron and his train were admitted within the walls of the fort and the heavy portcullis was let down behind them. The gloomy halls were lit up and the festive board groaned with dishes of food suited to the tastes of men who had acquired a keen appetite from a long journey in the open air. As the feasting and revelling proceeded, the lady embraced the first opportunity of making her cruel accusation against the unsuspecting youth. The baron listened to his lady and as he listened his wrath arose, till, frantic with rage, he pronounced the doom of the hapless Edward, which was that he was to perish without food in the lowest dungeon of the castle. As he pronounced the sentence, the first peal of thunder burst from the bosom of the clouds with an appalling crash over the battlements of the fortress and threatened to lay them in ruins. The guilty accuser trembled as when Heaven in judgement bears testimony against the deeds of the wicked. She clung, deadly pale, to the arm of her lord, whose voice, raised aloft, was heard above the raging of the tempest as he issued orders that Edward should be locked up immediately in the hold.

Poor Edward was hurried to his prison cell

Never was such an evening witnessed within the walls of Morton! The screaming of the lady – the shouting of the baron – the protests and pleading of Edward – the tumultuous voices of the company of men – the terrific roaring of the thunder, accompanied with lightning as vivid as if it would search through everyone's heart and reveal the secrets that lay hidden there. In the midst of the uproar, however, the baron's commands were performed and poor Edward was hurried to his prison cell.

The lady, having witnessed the accomplishment of her direful purpose, was now left to her own reflections, and these were anything but comfortable. If revenge had possessed her breast before, it was now replaced with remorse and she became the prey of a wretchedness that no tongue can express. She viewed herself as the base and traitorous murderer of an innocent and honourable youth, whose blood had already dyed her hands with a stain too foul ever to be washed out. The torture of her mind became excessive and all her worldly enjoyments lost their relish. In the night she was haunted by fearful dreams and the paleness and anxiety of her countenance indicated the torment and anxiety that preyed within.

Though the cause of her distress was known to none but herself, her friends and servants employed every means to recruit her wasted spirits. She frequently retired into the woods, and walked the pleasant lawns in the vicinity of the castle, to listen to the sound of the birds singing in the trees – but all was in vain.

It happened one day on her return from her solitary walk in the dell, that on entering the castle, she passed near the cell in which the victim of her cruelty was confined. From the low-grated window she heard him uttering many a deep and piteous moan, and, in the agony of his mind, bewailing his wretched fate. She paused for a moment and then hastened to her chamber. She called a confidential servant whom she secretly employed to carry food to the hopeless prisoner. The baron was to leave the castle in the morning and to be several days away from home. She expected that if she could keep Edward alive that on his return, when his anger had calmed down he might consent to release the injured youth. She did succeed in preserving his life in the dungeon, but it was only that he might die a more terrible death.

During the absence of the baron, the lady sought an interview with Agnes in the Carron woods, near her father's house. It was on one of the finest days of summer and Agnes had come out of the cottage to enjoy her solitary retreat in the woods. She had sat herself under her favourite tree which gently waved on the margin of the sparkling stream. It was a mountain ash – "a bonny rowan tree", richly clustered with downy blossoms spreading their fragrance on the breeze. Agnes sat on the green turf under the awning of its branches that screened her from the burning sun. While she plied her needle sewing, she sang a pleasant song with her silvery voice in unison with the soft humming of the mountain bees that had congregated in hundreds among the scented branches. The sporting trout leapt from the calm pool that spread itself like a polished mirror at her feet reflecting her own beautiful image. Despite the wonders of her tranquil surroundings she never noticed them as her thoughts were occupied with the form and features of her sweetheart. It was here that she and Edward often met and, being ignorant of his present plight, she imagined that even now he might be on his way to pay her a visit.

At this moment, the approach of someone was announced by the rustling of the undergrowth and the motion of the forest trees. Imagine her surprise when the lady of Morton stood before her! – but who was the more lady-like – the lowly maiden in the bloom of innocence and beauty, or the high-born dame, pale and agitated, and conscience smitten?

"Lady, what ails you?" was the question Agnes was about to ask after her first surprise was over, for she saw that grief and care were inmates of her bosom; and all the sympathies of her gentle and confiding heart were awakened. The lady, however, anticipated her and said, with an agonising energy of expression the reason for her errand. She informed her of the imprisonment of her lover, without explaining the reason and requested her to visit the castle on a particular day, to beg the baron for Edward's release.

As the timid deer, when struck in the heart with the huntsman's arrow, bounds into the thicket to bleed and die unseen, so Agnes, as if smitten by a startling apparition, staggered to her cottage to pour out the full gush of her grief in the bosom of her sympathising parents. Edward a prisoner in the deepest dungeon of the castle! For what conceivable crime could he be so rudely treated?

The time passed on heavily and Agnes waited with tormenting impatience the appointed day. She proceeded to the castle dressed in her best clothes and her timid heart was smitten with terror at the form of those dark towers looming in the distance. Within its gloomy walls her dearest love was confined. She was on the way to attempt to rescue her lover, but how were her gentle hands to tear apart the strong bars of his prison? Or how could her sorrowful pleading and begging move the heart of the gruff and surly baron?

On her arrival, the lady found a way to introduce Agnes to her lord, in whose presence she left her to do her best in pleading for Edward. The interview, however, was brief. No sooner was his name mentioned as still being alive than the baron swore a solemn oath that he should instantly die and that his death should not be a common one. Gentle Agnes' terror was extreme and she fled in haste from the face of the wrathful man, and without stopping, ran and hid herself in her cottage on the Carron.

The circumstances of Edward still being alive made the chieftain suspicious, as he knew that no one could survive so long without food. He interrogated his servants, but they all denied that they knew anything about it. Never the less, in his lordly arrogance he instantly put two of them to death as supposed traitors to their master. If two people, on mere suspicion could be thus unceremoniously despatched, we may easily conceive that the death of Edward was to be accompanied with circumstances of no ordinary cruelty.

The particular kind of death that the youth was to undergo soon suggested itself to the fierce mind of the haughty lord – to hang him from the highest tree on the lawn, or to shoot him through the heart with a barbed arrow, or to chop his head off, was, any one of them, a method of execution that was too lenient and speedy for such a notorious criminal. Instead he decreed that he should be drawn to death at the heels of furious horses. For this purpose, the wildest and untameable animals were to be sought, so that the execution might be as cruel as possible.

Two fierce and unruly horses were found grazing in a nearby wood and these were caught for the purpose of accomplishing the deed. In order to make the spirited animals as furious as possible, a pair of spurs was attached to each by a strap passing round the body. That way the sharp rowels would plunge into their sides with every step they took and impel them forward with the speed of an arrow.

Edward was brought from his cell and laid on his back on the ground. Strong ropes that were tied to the horses were then bound round his neck and shoulders. The animals were then led a short distance from the castle gate, when, being lashed with whips, they galloped across the fields, dragging at their heels the screaming victim. The spurs, like the flapping of wings on their impatient sides, goaded them to madness.

The horses sped in the direction of Durisdeer village and within a short distance of it the head was torn from the body. Their race lasted nearly three miles before this catastrophe occurred. At this point they turned and sped in the southerly direction to where the Kirk Burn joins the Carron, and having entered the mouth of its deep and narrow channel, they were cornered and caught by country people who had assembled in sorrowful groups to witness the scene. The shattered body was disentangled from the ropes by which it was bound and carried back to the place where the head was lying, and buried on the spot.

The report of Edward's cruel death struck the heart of Agnes with a deadly stroke and she instantly died in the arms of her parents. The cottage was filled with grief and nothing was heard in the neighbourhood but expressions of sorrow. She was buried on the green beside her lover at a place that was given the name of "The Heads" and a rough memorial stone was placed to mark the grave of the "Martyr Lovers".

When the lady was told about Edward's death and all its attendant circumstances, the report fell upon her spirit like the fiery bolt of heaven upon the trees of the forest. It blighted all her heart and withered all her joy. Pale, emaciated and horror-struck, she sat alone in the gloomy halls of the castle. At length the agony of her mind reached such a pitch that she was forced to confess her crime. In the middle of the rebukes of her friends and the accusations of her conscience, she lost her reason. She was sent to a lonely apartment where she eventually died in a most pitiful state.

The punishment that the conscience inflicts on the guilty is frequently worse than any punishment inflicted by human laws.

The punishment that the conscience inflicts on the guilty is frequently worse than any punishment inflicted by human hand.

Chapter 2
Weird stories of ghosts, witches and fairies

The Bank Wood near Kirkconnel no longer exists, but it had the reputation of being haunted. It was a strip of natural wood on the left bank of the Nith about half-a-mile south of Kirkconnel village. In the days before the railway was constructed it was the terror of travellers who were obliged to pass through it at night. The growth of trees in that wood was thick and close, and, with the road running through the centre it was anything but a pleasant place on a dark night. Cases of highway robbery were frequent there, and it was even whispered that darker deeds had been perpetrated within its shades.

An evil place at night, the Bank Wood was even shunned in broad daylight. Its closely set undergrowth afforded shelter and hiding to tramps and bad characters of which there were too many going about in those days.

Here are some of the stories about the Bank Wood that were told in the early 1800s:

A resident of Kirkconnel went into the wood one day to cut down a tree for firewood. He was just about to begin his task, when, suddenly and without warning, a black man appeared as if from the earth. He placed his hand on the tree and clearly showed by gestures that the work of destruction would not be allowed to proceed. Terrified of the apparition, for such he judged it, the woodcutter stopped and hurried off home as quick as his legs would carry him, sparing the tree.

One dark night in 1850 a man was on his way from Kirkconnel to Sanquhar. He had crossed Polveoch Burn and reached the middle of the road when he heard a sound as if a carriage drawn by a pair of horses was coming down the road at what he reckoned was an easy trot. He continued walking on, till the sound came so near that he could plainly hear the breathing of horses and the creaking of the harness. Thinking the horses and carriage would run him over he stepped to the roadside to allow them to pass. He then looked round, but to his amazement he saw nothing, nor did he again hear a sound. All around was still. No carriage or vehicle of any kind passed him on his way to Sanquhar, and no one, he afterwards learned, had seen one pass through Kirkconnel that night.

Weird faces were wont to peep in at the windows

Similar mysterious noises were also heard from time to time by others, as well as a clanking sound as if heavy chains were being dragged about.

Ghost stories are common enough in Upper Nithsdale. It is well known that Kirkconnel in Tynron was a haunted house. Weird faces, with grinning teeth and fiery eyes were wont to peep in at the windows on winter evenings. Eldritch sounds and low moaning proceeded in the darkness from the copse around. Indeed, had there not been a considerable use made of cast horse shoes, of rowan branches cut when no eye saw the cutter, of "fow" (leeks) growing on the thatch, and a careful observance paid to certain new moons and other duties, life would hardly have been worth living in that lonely sheiling. Satan himself was once seen sitting on the bridge that crosses the dark defile near it, but, scared, he fled beneath the starlight noiselessly down into the deep recess.

The Devil, in different forms and disguises was said to be seen in the Bank Wood and on stormy nights liked to sit on a rock playing the bagpipes. Accidents were frequent in that neighbourhood and, rightly or wrongly, the Devil was blamed for having a share in them.

A farmer and his wife were driving home from Sanquhar when near that stone the horse took fright, bolted and upset the gig, killing the wife. The Devil got the blame for frightening the horse.

About 14 miles downstream, near Thornhill where the Nith Bridge now stands, there was originally only a ford, which was passed by boat, giving name still to the Boat Brae on the Thornhill side.

The necessity of a bridge was proved to the county by a melancholy accident which took place on the evening of a Thornhill Candlemass Fair, 23rd February, 1773, when 6 people out of 13 were drowned by the upsetting of the boat. The following were the names of those who met their sad fate, and it will be observed that there were three men with the name "James" and three women called "Jean". They were:- James Ferguson, farmer from Glenwhargen; James Geddes, blacksmith from Knowkelly, Tynron; James Gracie, Penfilan, Keir; Jean Kirkpatrick, Penfilan, Keir; Jean Rorison from Moniaive and Jean Hairstens, Moniaive.

The boatman was William Fingland who was saved by his son Thomas who was riding across on the horse of James Gracie, and was just in time to save his father.

The boat was upset by a gust of wind, but the superstitious ascribed the accident to other causes.

It got abroad that a strange man, who "smelled of sulphur" rushed into the boat as it was pushing off and that he went down with the boat never to be seen again. That, to some, inferred that an agent of Satan had brought about the catastrophe.

James Ferguson of Glenwhargen was remarkable for his strength and it was supposed that he must have been kept down by the death struggles of the women.

In those days money could not be raised by the county as readily as at present, and much of the funds had to be raised by voluntary subscriptions. The bridge was thus not built till 1777.

Then there is the story of the old man who directed the singing in Glencairn Church who died in the late 1800s. He was out one moonlit evening in the garden in meditative mood, when he heard a sound, as if a cart containing pieces of metal had been tilted up and the materials discharged. He believed that a murdered infant had been buried in that garden and that this was its ghost manifesting itself.

Murdered innocents were also frequently heard wailing in the mid-1800s in the corn and in the thickets around Macqueston in Tynron. A gentleman of suspect morality had occupied that house earlier in the century. So troublesome were these sounds that for a while the new tenant had great difficulty in retaining servants.

Then there is the tale of a young dairy maid who lived in a haunted house at Kirkconnel, in Tynron Glen, in the early 1800s. At night strange faces peered in at the window and "eldritch" laughter was heard. Her father once saw a red figure at dusk on the ledge of the bridge near the house which appeared of human shape, but disappeared as he approached.

Perhaps the best documented ghost was the one reported in the Sunday Post of 14 August, 1977.

Lloyd Richards and his wife were spending a holiday with Mrs Richard's family in the village of Leadhills in Lanarkshire.

One day Lloyd, whose home was in Liverpool, was walking alone in the Lowther Hills above Wanlockhead when a mist came down, though it was midsummer. Suddenly, out of the mist, came a young woman dressed in strange clothes, carrying a wicker basket. She seemed distressed. As Lloyd went towards her, he heard her say, "Look in the stones!", but before he could reach her, she had disappeared into the mist. Lloyd told the family about the strange encounter.

They told him that 100 years earlier, a young girl called Jenny Miller set out to walk over the hills from Kirkhope Farm, where she worked, to her sister's wedding at Wanlockhead. As she crossed the hills, she was caught

The strange figure said "Look in the stones"

in a blizzard and stumbled into the workings of an old lead mine. Her body was found there a few days later.

The locals built a cairn on the spot. On a piece of stone they carved the words "In memoriam, Jenny Miller 1877". The cairn still stood, but the inscription had disappeared. Intrigued, Lloyd and his brothers-in-law, Douglas and Tom Cowell, set out to find the cairn. Sure enough, there it was by the old lead mine. Then Lloyd remembered what the strange figure had said, "Look in the stones". One by one he searched through the rocks in the cairn – and buried there, in two halves, he found the stone bearing Jenny's name.

The stone is now in the mining museum at Wanlockhead. Just one more winter in the open would have obliterated the faint inscription. It is said that from time to time anglers in the hills report that they too have seen the figure of a girl in the mountain mist.

There are numerous tales of witches in Upper Nithsdale and I have already chronicled the antics of a famous coven of them that lived in Crawick in my book "Old Sanquhar Tales".

A young farmer from Closeburn was carting stones from a neighbouring quarry when his horse came to a standstill opposite a witch's door. Two other carters passed him and jeered at both the witch and the youth. The witch, to whom he had always been civil, came forward and with a slight push, adjusted the ponderous stone that had slipped and was stopping the wheel. "Now, go", she said, "thou wilt find them at the gate below Gilchristland". At that very spot he found the perplexed carters standing, both horses trembling and sweating, so that he easily went past them and reached his goal first.

There was a small loch on Blackchub farm in the parish of Penpont that was 120 yards in length and 70 yards in breadth before it was extended for wildfowling. It was called the Dow Dhu, or Black Loch as the words signify in Gaelic and its waters were reputed to have extraordinary healing powers.

It wasn't necessary that the person, or animal subjected to the spell of witchcraft should visit the loch. This might have involved considerable hazard, so the prudent alternative of employing a deputy was often adopted. To accomplish the desired end the deputy was required to observe certain rules. He had to carry a part of the clothes of the person or the furniture of the animal bewitched as an offering to the spirit of the loch. When the person reached it he had to draw water in a vessel, which on no account had to touch the ground, turn himself round with the sun, and to throw his offering to the spirit over his left shoulder. He then had to carry the water to the sick person or animal without once looking back.

All this had to be done in absolute silence and the messenger had to salute no one on the way.

Our forebears in the olden days believed that fairies had such power and influence over mortals that the greatest care possible was taken not to give them offence in any way. Hence, they were always spoken of with respect and in a kindly manner termed the "good little folks".

Fairies have long been associated with Upper Nithsdale and I have already written about the Sanquhar fairies in "Old Sanquhar Tales". In it, I recounted how they gambolled in Sanquhar on the "Fairy Knowe" that overlooks the "Waird", or how they frequented the banks of Euchan.

There is a curious, natural knoll at Carronbridge, also known as Fairy Knowe. There, about 150 years ago, a cow happened to be grazing on the top of the knowe when her foot went down through an urn. The urn was about 16 inches tall and contained bones, but it fell to pieces when it was exposed to the air.

The gardens at Drumlanrig Castle were also reputed to have been visited by fairies. They were often seen dancing in a nearby glade, but Kirkconnel boasts a wonderful tale of the "little folk".

The brae of Polveoch, at the west end of Bank Wood, was a favourite meeting place of the fairies. Here the good little folks assembled on May Day to celebrate the advent of summer. Groups came in from Kello Water, Glen Aylmer and Glen Wharry. When all had gathered together they rode merrily over the knowes towards the Bale Hill. It was said that there on the slopes that faced the sun a beautiful doorway would open for them, which they entered, two at a time, with the green turf closing over the last pair to get in.

Halloween was another of their gala nights. It was said that one Halloween two farm servants, while on their way to Todholes to see their sweethearts, heard sounds of most enchanting music coming from Polveoch Burn. Turning aside to discover where it was coming from, they were astonished to see in a glade among the trees a company of male and female fairies dancing to a band of pipers. They were all dressed in the most elegant style, and their delicate little bodies swirled in a fashion that entranced the awestruck lads.

One, however, thought the strange sight could bode no good and he beat a hasty retreat, leaving his companion gazing admiringly on the dazzling show. For a long time he stood and feasted his eyes and ears on the exquisite scene and the beautiful melody until his presence was discovered by one of the company and he was invited to take part in the dance and presented with fruit and wine. He daringly accepted and the refreshments seemed to put a new life into him. He joined in the dance

A company of fairies danced to a band of pipers

with great zest and was so good that the little ladies in green made quite a hero of him and did all in their power to make him enjoy himself.

Drinking the fairies' wine caused him to lose all calculation of time and twelve months went by with the young fellow still enjoying himself with the wee folks. The following Halloween he was found at the same place by his companion who offended the fairies by refusing a drink that was offered to him. He broke the spell that bound his friend by grabbing hold of him and pulling him away. The poor chap could scarcely believe that he had been twelve months with the fairies and said that the time only seemed like an hour or two. Ever after he was endowed with second sight.

Chapter 3
Wraiths and premonitions

Wraiths differ from ghosts in that they are apparitions in the likeness of people still living and are supposed to be seen either at the time of the death of the person whose likeness is seen, or immediately before. Some strange stories are told of these mysterious appearances. The following are well authenticated cases.

Joseph Black, a miner who lived at Grievehill, near New Cumnock regularly attended the North U.P. Church in Sanquhar. Notwithstanding the fact that going and returning from his home to the church entailed a walk of close on twenty miles, his seat in church was seldom empty. He generally attended both the morning and evening services, so that his homeward journey was nearly always performed in the dark.

On the last occasion that he attended the evening service he set out for home as usual. The greater part of his way was by the public road. It was a fine, moonlit night and all went well with him for the first two miles. After he passed Gateside farm and was nearing what was known as the "Brunt Houses" (near Wellstrand), he became aware of a man, or rather the likeness of a man, walking alongside of him. He hadn't noticed his approach, nor did he hear any footsteps, and the apparition moved along with a mysterious gliding motion.

Black at first thought that it must be his own shadow, but a moment was sufficient to show that it could not be so, as the mysterious man was between him and the moon. Although alarmed at being in such strange company, he didn't lose his presence of mind, but observed that the figure was the exact double of him in size, build and dress, even to the bonnet and plaid. This apparition continued to accompany him as far as the Bank Wood, when it disappeared as unaccountably as it came, and without having spoken or made a sound, or sign of any kind.

Black, although alarmed, continued his journey, and arriving home safely told his wife about the strange likeness of himself that had accompanied him part of the way. The couple then had supper and went to bed, but were only a short while asleep when they were suddenly awakened by a loud crash as if a part of the house had fallen down. They got up in great alarm and looked all over the place, but could see nothing amiss, nor anything that could in any way account for the noise.

The house in which they lived consisted of a single apartment with two built-in beds and was furnished as working peoples' generally were, with tables, chairs, cupboard and crockery rack. After examining the house inside and out and finding nothing wrong, they returned to their bed hoping not to be disturbed again.

They had not yet fully fallen asleep when another crash came, this time as if a cupboard and crockery rack, with all the crockery in the house, had been dashed in the middle of the floor. Again getting up and striking a light, they were more than ever amazed to find everything in its proper place. Nothing had been touched, and although another search round was made, no clue could be found as to the cause. It being close on their usual rising time, Black and his wife did not go back to bed, but took some breakfast together, and after praying, he went out to his daily toil.

The place Black worked at was entered by a "level" and there being no mining regulations in those days, the miners could go to and from their work as best it suited them selves.

Joseph Black had got to his workplace alright and started his work when he was suddenly buried under a heavy fall from the roof. There he lay more dead than alive, until he was discovered later on in the morning by the man who worked next to him. When he was taken out, it was found that his back was broken and he only lived for a short time. His widow often talked of her husband having walked with his own wraith and of the mysterious noises heard on the eve of her bereavement.

Then there is the tale of a man called Peter Hastie who lived in the Lochan, Sanquhar who saw a remarkable apparition when he was a youth. He had been brought up in Kirkconnel and had a school friend called Thomas Blacklock, who, like himself, went to work on a farm after leaving school. Blacklock started work at Nether Cairn, while Hastie started at Kelloside, a distance of two miles separating the places.

One day in spring Hastie was engaged in carting manure from the farm steading to one of the fields near the public road. About one o'clock, when he was going with his first load after lunch he saw, just before he reached the gate, his friend Thomas Blacklock coming down the road to meet him, which made him wonder what could be bringing him here at that time of day.

Being by this time at the gate leading into the field, Hastie caught hold of the bridle to lead the horse in, but the beast was startled at something. One of the wheels struck the gate post upsetting the cart, and Hastie narrowly escaped it falling on him.

The people in the field, on seeing his predicament, ran to his assistance and quickly put things to rights. His friend Blackwood, however, instead of lending a hand, stood quietly looking on. Hastie couldn't understand his lack of action in view of the fact they were close friends, but being busy at the time he only gave the matter a passing thought. Once everything was put right again he looked round for his friend, but he was nowhere to be seen, nor had any of the field workers seen him.

That evening, when returning from their work, Hastie and his fellow workers were met by a man from the Cairn who told them that that day at about one o'clock Thomas Blacklock had been accidentally killed.

It appears that at Nether Cairn Blacklock had, like his friend, been carting manure. He had taken a load after lunch and was in the act of returning, sitting on the empty cart, when the horse took fright, ran away and threw him out. His head struck a large stone and he was killed on the spot. The time of Thomas Blacklock's tragic death corresponded exactly with the time Peter Hastie saw the appearance of his old companion and when he himself had an accident with his own cart.

Premonitions, like wraiths are phenomena that are not easy to explain or understand. James Hogg, the Ettrick Shepherd, who was, for a while, a tenant of Laight farm in the parish of Tynron on the banks of the Scaur, refers to an omen called the "death bell". It was a tingling in the ears that was believed to announce a friend's death. Just as the "light before death" – which can only be seen by one at a time – so, the death bell can only be heard by one person at a time.

Thomas Blacklock was killed when he was thrown out of his cart

An old woman in Cairn Valley once witnessed the premonitory light, which lit up the interior of the byre while she was engaged milking her cows and she later learned that her mother who resided some miles distant had expired that evening.

A Nithsdale shepherd, seeing a light from a distance, rushed in a state of great agitation into a neighbouring cottage, which happened to be near, and brought out the man of the house. Both thought that it must have been the "light which is seen before death", but the mistress of the house soothed them by remarking that such a light could not be seen by two at once.

The grandfather of a lady in Tynron dreamed he was at a ball with his sister who appeared in a white dress. She left the ballroom saying to him, "you will not be long in following me". She died a short time later and he died soon afterwards.

Then there is the tale of the house maid to a medical man in Moniaive in the early 1800s who frequently heard strange foot-falls in an upper room. After a while the doctor suddenly took ill, lay down on the sofa and died over the very spot on the floor where those alarming foot-falls had been most frequently heard.

The relations of a gentleman who lived in Tynron were warned of death by the sound of wheels upon the gravel walk leading to the door, when no wheels were there, while a family in Durisdeer were regularly warned by a swishing sound against the panes of the window.

The Kirkpatrick family were persuaded in ancient times, that when a death was to take place in the family, a swan always made its appearance on Closeburn Castle Loch that at one time all but surrounded the castle, until it was finally completely drained in 1859. The last omen of this nature on record saddened the nuptials of Sir Thomas, the first baronet, when marrying for the third time.

On the day of the wedding, his son Roger went out of the castle, and, happening to turn his eyes towards the loch, saw the fatal bird. Returning overwhelmed with melancholy his father rallied him on his despondent appearance, alleging his new stepmother to be the cause of his sadness, when the young man answered: "Perhaps ere long you may also be sorrowful". He expired that night.

Chapter 4
Wakes and funerals

In the bleak upland district between Sanquhar and Muirkirk there stood about two hundred and seventy years ago, midway between the ancient burgh and the "Church in the Moors", the sheiling of Lagminnan.

It occupied a lonely spot among the dreary, uninviting hills and was very remote with no other houses nearby. The dwelling consisted of a humble "but and ben" and was a very ordinary building. Its walls were built of rough whinstones, dug from the hillside, while the roof was formed of trees cut from the neighbouring wood, thatched with heather which grew in abundance all round about and ridged with tough divots of bent grass.

The larger of the two rooms was a big one that was used as the kitchen. It had a built-in bed, meal cupboard, plate rack, long settle and other crude but substantial furnishings. The fireplace was in the middle of the floor, the smoke from which hung lazily overhead. It smoked the hams that hung in the rafters before finally escaping to the open air through a hole in the thatch that served the purpose of chimney.

The man of the house was referred to as "Lagminnan" after the name of his sheiling. Both he and his father before him had been born there. He had spent his whole life among his native hills and had never wandered more than twenty miles from his home. Here he grew from youth to age, if not a hermit, at least a canny old bachelor.

His only companion was his housekeeper, Marjory who was nearly as old as himself and his two collie dogs that helped him to take care of his livestock. They consisted of two cows, a stirk, a score of sheep and a couple of pet lambs, all of which occupied the byre and outhouse that stood at the end of the house.

At the time of this tale Lagminnan was eighty-years-old, his tall form had become bent and his step feeble. At length he went the way of all flesh and died, much to the grief of his faithful old housekeeper. As all his friends were dead, Marjory was the only one left to mourn his loss.

On hearing of his death, a number of young men and women from the neighbouring cottages went to Lagminnan to keep the old woman company and "wake" the corpse. That was done by sitting in the room where the body lay, day and night until the funeral took place.

Things went well enough for the first couple of nights. After the housekeeper went to bed several girls took over and kept watch by the side of the corpse till morning. On the night before the funeral old Marjory went to the house of a neighbour, leaving the body of her master in charge of six or eight young women.

She hadn't been long gone when an equal number of young men put in an appearance. They brought with them a plentiful supply of whisky and other good things with which to pleasantly pass the long hours of night.

Soon the glass and song went merrily round, until the "mirth and fun grew fast and furious". A dance was proposed, and as readily agreed to. They managed to play some sort of music and were soon dancing merrily. When their fun and frolic was at its height, a dreadful thing happened – the dead man, dressed in his grave clothes, sprang out of the bed, and with his glassy eyes staring at the revellers, stood leaning against the end of the bed. Had a thunderbolt or a bombshell fallen in their midst it could not have caused greater panic. Every man and woman present was seized by terror and it became a case of "de'il tak the hindmost" as they all made a mad rush for outside. The bed in which the

"de'il tak the hind most"

corpse had lain was close to the door, and as each individual made his or her exit, it was with a bound and a yell as they were all terrified in case the dead man should clutch and devour them. When they did get outside, most of them ran without stopping till they reached their own homes, where they told of the awful thing that had happened at Lagminnan.

Soon the whole countryside was made aware of the startling occurrence, and by break of day a large number of folk gathered at a short distance from the house, although none had enough courage to enter it.

Broad daylight, however, often dispels many a strange thing seen in the dark. When the sun was well up in the east several of the more courageous ventured forward to the house and looked in at the window. There they saw the corpse standing with its feet on the floor, leaning against the end of the bed, in the exact position it had occupied when the revellers beat their hasty retreat.

Long they looked and watched, but the dead man still kept his ground, never moving a muscle. At last two or three of the boldest ventured inside, and on making an inspection saw how the whole thing had happened.

The bed where the corpse was laid was low and supported by rungs. A large dog which accompanied one of the young men had crawled under it and fallen asleep. When it was suddenly awakened by the noise of the dancers it had risen to its full height. Being a powerful animal, it had lifted the bed on its back, the corpse had slid over the end, the feet had come to the floor and the body being stiff it had stood there.

Things were soon put to rights and old Lagminnan was decently "kisted" and as decently buried beside his fathers in the old kirkyard of Kirkconnel in Glen Aylmer. The story of Lagminnan's wake was the cause of many a hearty laugh for many a day.

Doctor Rob Allison regularly attended wakes and funerals. He and his wife Meg was a curious pair of worthies who lived in Sanquhar and many a droll story was told about them.

Rob had served in the Royal Navy as a young man and had fought in many sea battles. On being discharged from the navy he returned to his native burgh to live and married Meg McCall. Having served an apprenticeship as a shoemaker in his youth he set up in business as a cobbler. He also claimed to be able to cure sick pigs and on account of this talent was nicknamed "The Doctor", a title of which he was rather proud.

He was well known all over the district and was also a noted storyteller. While his hands were busily employed patching a pair of old shoes he was likely to talk at length about the wonders he had seen on foreign shores and the part he had played in the wars against the French and Spanish. His workshop was the nightly haunt of the youth of the town who thoroughly enjoyed an hour's crack with the old veteran.

Some wag or other had said that at the battle of Cape Saint Vincent the Doctor had hidden in one of the ship's copper tanks used for storing fresh water. Although usually of a quiet, good-natured disposition, this was a challenge to his honour he could not stand – his blood rebelled at the name of coward. Knowing how to provoke him, the boys would torment him for fun by going to his door and shouting "Copper Kettle" and other nicknames. On these occasions it didn't matter what he was doing, everything was cast aside and he would chase after the boys throwing at them a stone, hammer or whatever first came to hand.

As mentioned earlier, the Doctor regularly attended all the funerals in the district and whether invited or not, wet or dry, he was sure to be there. His presence on these solemn occasions was not so much to show respect to the departed as to partake of the refreshments that were liberally dispatched at these events, and no funeral was worth speaking about if he did not get "roarin' fu'".

The Doctor's partiality for funerals was well known. He was occasionally made the subject of a hoax by being invited to witness the burial of someone who wasn't dead, so that more than once he received a shock by meeting on the road the person whose funeral he was going to.

Eventually a change took place. The unseemly doings that occurred all too frequently at funerals called for intervention and a public meeting was held in the Council House. There it was decided to do away with the entertainment except for one round at the lifting and another when returning from the kirkyard. This arrangement sorely displeased the Doctor, who, being invited to a funeral a few days afterwards, looked sternly at the person inviting him and said: "Wha the de'il do ye think's gaun to change their claes for only twae glass o' whisky? They may keep her till she rots". It was said that he rarely, if ever, was seen at any funerals afterwards.

Post Office Row, Wanlockhead c1880

The village of Wanlockhead lies at the north-east corner of the parish of Sanquhar. It derives its existence from the lead mines that have been worked from an early period. The miners' houses lie for the most part round the base of the Dod Hill, from which the inhabitants were frequently nicknamed the "Dodders".

In early times the dead were carried all the way from Wanlockhead to Sanquhar for interment, either by Glendyne or Mennock and the scenes on such occasions were frequently far from edifying or solemnising. Inhabitants from surrounding parishes were drafted to share in the interment till a graveyard was obtained at Meadowfoot on the Wanlock about 230 years ago, although, unusually there was no gravedigger. This last office used to be performed by the family of the deceased working in partnerships of usually four members. Fortunately there were usually enough family members, as the people of Wanlockhead were all closely related as a result of inter-marriage.

It is interesting to note that it was the custom in Scotland in earlier days to dress the body of the deceased in a white shroud, or "mort cloths" as they were called. One of the last Acts of the old Scottish Parliament in 1707 was designed to protect the Scottish woollen industry from linen and cheap imported cotton calicoes from India, but led to the practice of exhuming the deceased. This strange act decreed that burial shrouds should be made of wool. It stipulated that "no corpse of any person of

St John's Church, Wanlockhead c1880

what condition or quality whatsoever shall be buried in linen and that – plain woollen cloth or stuff shall only be made use of in all time coming". The saying "pulling the wool over their eyes" is probably derived from that practice of covering the dead with a woollen shroud so that all was concealed.

As a way of getting round the Act, the canny Scots reasoned that the body did not have to remain buried in a woollen shroud, so the practice evolved of exhuming the body to recover the mort cloth and rent it out again.

While the Scots have a long tradition of paying due respect to their dead, the same has not always been the case for those who committed suicide among their midst.

On the summit of the Lowthers, overlooking Wanlockhead, where the counties of Dumfries and Lanark meet, as also the lands of the three lairds at the time – the Duke of Buccleuch, the Earl of Hopetoun and Mr Irving of Newton – and here, owing to a superstitious feeling, it was the custom up until about the middle of the nineteenth century to bury suicides. Being on the edge of two counties and the borders of three lairds' lands it was supposed that the spot could legally be claimed by none as the boundaries of the properties had never been clearly defined.

Dr John Brown in his interesting paper entitled "Enterkin", says: "The bodies were brought from great distances all round, and, in accordance with the dark superstitions of the time, the unblessed corpse was treated with curious indignity – no dressing with mort cloths, no striking (binding) of the pitiful limbs – the body was thrust with the clothes it was found in into a rude box, not even shaped like a coffin, and hurried away on some old shattered cart or sledge with ropes for harness.

"One can imagine the miserable procession as it slunk, often during night, through the villages and past the farmsteads, everyone turning from it as abhorred. Then arrived at this high and desolate region, the horse was taken out and the weary burden dragged with pain up to its resting place and carried head foremost as in contempt. Then a shallow hole dug and the long, uncouth box pushed in – the cart and harness were left to rot as accursed.

"The white human bones may sometimes be seen among the thick, short grass". He goes on to recall with a shudder on seeing one that had been there for more than fifty years: "Coming – when crossing that hill top – upon a small outstretched hand, as if one crying from the ground. This one little hand, with its thin fingers held up to heaven, as if in agony of supplication or despair. What a sight seen against the spotless sky, or crossing the disc of the waning moon?"

The horror of seeing a hand with its thin fingers pointing to heaven

There is a tradition that Burke and Hare, the notorious grave-robbers used to lodge at Stake Moss, just above Wanlockhead, to retrieve those miserable wretches under cover of darkness, to be taken for dissection on the surgeons' tables in Edinburgh. It is also interesting to note that the Stake Moss got its name from the horrible practice that was sometimes carried out, of impaling the corpse of a suicide at burial on a stake.

Dr James Laurie, a native of Dunscore, was one of the surgeons who courageously attended those stricken with cholera in the dreadful outbreak in Dumfries in 1832. He went on to become a teacher and was headmaster of the Crichton School in Sanquhar for 33 years.

Dr Laurie had been a medical student during the terrible Burke and Hare times, and he used to describe the scene of Burke's execution in Edinburgh on the morning of 28 January, 1829, at which he was present, and the horrid hideousness of which he never forgot.

He would depict in terrible graphic detail the immense crowd of people, calculated at forty thousand, who had assembled from all parts. He told how folk seethed round the scaffold and how they cheered the workmen when, after working all night in drizzling rain, they put the finishing touches to the grim structure. He described how the crowd made themselves hoarse with a terrific outburst of hootings and curses as Burke,

Crichton School, Sanquhar c1910

with the hangman and a Roman Catholic priest, made his appearance on the stroke of eight. Referring to one of Burke's victims some of the crowd cried out, "Dae ye see Daft Jamie's ghost?", whilst others shouted, "Auld Nick'll sune hae ye noo!" and so on.

Then he would describe what occurred after the body had been cut down and removed to the dissection room. How those students not belonging to the anatomy class clamoured to see it, and the riotous events that succeeded. He would conclude by describing how, at the end of the dissection, the general public were admitted in a stream of sixty folk a minute to view the corpse of the evil one as it lay naked and repulsive on the cold marble slab. It was a ghastly business and little wonder Dr Laurie could recall it all so vividly.

Chapter 5
A local Samson

Penpont is generally believed to have derived its name from a hanging bridge (from the Latin Pendous Pons) across the river Scaur that separated one part of it from the adjoining parish of Tynron.

High are the hills of Penpont, broad are their shoulders and tough is the whinstone that composes them. Broad also were the shoulders of many of its parishioners in olden times. The quantity of cubic air that their lungs could contain was enormous and the muscular development was a thing for which many were thankful.

The raw material of the soldier abounded in Scaur Glen, in the straths overlooked by Glenwhargen and in the soft undulating valleys that roll away from the base of Cairnkinna.

Thin-blooded tailors were reared in towns on sweaty systems in badly ventilated houses. Shopkeepers, light and wiry, with swift wagging tongues, leaped the counters like kangaroos, or ascended little ladders among soft goods with the agility of squirrels. Pale mechanics, pale preachers and

Penpont High Street c1920

teachers, with sour looks and sourer stomachs, fed on sago and arrowroot, tea and tobacco, to whom the haggis, immortalised by Robert Burns, eaten before going to bed was as heavy as a nightmare upon their groaning breasts – these were the civilians. He whom Burns celebrated as the "laird of the Cairn and Scaur" and won the world-renowned whistle, would, for strength of digestive ability, tested by John Barleycorn, have drunk blind a whole suburb of weavers.

But the mightiest production of Penpont parish was a local Samson, John McCall of Glenmanna that neighbours Glenwhargen. Although he was only six feet tall, his shoulders were as broad as a barn door and his limbs were moulded of iron. His clothes of hodden-grey were loosely fitted as if to allow for still greater growth, while his bonnet lay softly and kindly on his head. His huge oak-staff was like a weaver's beam and the grasp of his hand was like the embrace given you by the coming together of the top and bottom millstones.

The young clergy man, newly inducted into Penpont felt to his cost the warmth and pressure of Glenmanna's squeeze. He had finished his sermon and was quite exhausted by his exertions. He was a thin and emaciated man and looked remarkably like a subject for delicate ladies to revive by means of cakes and wine when he came tripping forward to respond to that mark of respect usual on such occasions – namely, the shaking of hands.

Folk of all ranks and both sexes thronged forward for the salutation. There was a rustling and a hustling. The fragrance of musk and the smell of boiled turnips mingled around the preachers head, shedding a curious kind of incense on the ceremony, and the squeezing to get forward was quite exciting. Among the first, by sheer strength, was Glenmanna. He was gallant enough however, to give way to a lady whose jewelled fingers were a strong contrast to the hand of the Samson-like shepherd. The preacher had scarcely time to mark the "new suit of hodden-grey, the red and blue striped plaid, the black wool "rig and fur" galligaskins (loose fitting breeches) on the legs, each formed with a long stripe to cover the upper parts of the foot and linked by two holes over his third and fourth toes, when his hand was in that of Glenmanna.

Now, McCall, though strong as Goliath, was innocent as a dove and almost unaware of his own firmness of muscle. The preacher too, had struck him as a decent type, so he heartily rocked to and fro the pulpy fingers, assuring their owner that he wished him the best of luck. He told him that sitting under him would likely be a pleasure and that he "maun gie him a ca' sune, or they would be owre head and ears wi' the clippin". Meantime the minister felt as if his mouth was filled with cayenne pepper.

Tears starting from his eyes, the preacher gazed on his fingers after the fierce encounter and found blood coming from beneath every nail. He crammed all four into his mouth and hurried out of the churchyard without any more shaking of hands. As for Glenmanna, he had the proud conscience of doing his duty and mingled with the crowd quite unaware of the torture he had administered. No wonder when people usually met honest John of Upper Penpont, they thrust only their forefinger, cocked like a pistol, into his palm extended to salute them.

Glenmanna easily threw the stranger

On one occasion, Glenmanna was returning from Edinburgh when a stranger, struck by his appearance, inquired if he had a taste for wrestling. "Some, but no very meikle", replied Glenmanna. "I'll tie my horse to this alder tree", said the stranger, who was a well-knit fellow, with something genteel in his appearance, "and let us try a throw or two on this soft meadow". Glenmanna gave a half-willing ascent. They were equal in height, but the stranger, though what he wanted in bone appeared to be compensated by activity. The stranger, in shorter time than we take to tell it, was placed in that position in which:

"The tip of the toes and the point of the nose

Look up to the sky like the daises".

"My opinion of Scotland has risen with my fall", said the stranger, "and in reply to your question, I say, no, I want no more wrestling, but I want to know your name". "Ye wud wunner what's in Scotland", said

Glenmanna, "but I, Jock McCall, reside at Glenmanna, a tenant of the Duke of Queensberry".

The stranger on the other hand, announced himself as Viscount Kenmure. Glenmanna at once ducked and took his bonnet off, begging pardon for his impudence in "warsling wi' sic a great man, but that it was an accidental sin". Ever after, Kenmure and the rustic shepherd had a warm feeling towards each other and met like friends on equal terms, for the Viscount practised and admired the manly art of self-defence.

James, Duke of Queensberry, resolved to astonish the Cockneys with the strength of his shepherd. So, amid a number of trained men, proud of their prowess, he announced that he could bring a raw recruit – a shepherd from his Scottish estates – who would turn out to be more than a match for the nerve and sinews of London.

The test game chosen was that of putting or throwing the stone. Some large bets were staked, chiefly against the Duke, who lost no time in writing to John McCall, to whom his request was like that of an Emperor, brooking no refusal.

The material to be thrown was a large ball of lead, and the place was a bowling green or cricket field in the Metropolis, surrounded by a high wall. Out strutted the English champion with the bluster of the turkey and the peacock's pride, looking as sprightly as possible, and suggesting ideas connected with Glenmanna's bonnet, galligaskins, stiff appearance and uncombed hair. That caused the spectators to titter much at the shepherd and to look on him as some clown or clumsy follower of the Duke, brought forward to jest. Glenmanna didn't hear their laughter, for his soul was directed towards the champion and towards his own mission for which he had travelled so far.

"Thud" landed his opponent's ball right up against the wall amid a perfect explosion of applause. While hats were tossing, Glenmanna, urged on by a whisper from the Duke, was screwing up every muscle to its proper pitch, though affecting the greatest care in his manner.

"Will you throw off your coat? It will give you greater freedom", said His Grace. "Coat for that", replied Glenmanna, "I guessed it was to be some great sky-rocket o' a throw that I was brocht a' the way to London to see – something that I could hae thocht on a' the way gain' hame. Na! Na! Nae coat aff for that. Ye micht hae done't yoursel'". Then poising the ball a short while in his hand, and repeating as by way of incantation over it,

"Auld man o' Maybole,
Can ye shoe a wee foal?
Yes indeed, and that I can,
Just as weel as any man".

Then he suddenly let it fly. "There", he cried, "and he that likes may gang and fetch it back". The ball curved forward as if shot from the mouth of a cannon, cleared the wall by a few inches and landed on the tile roof of a house beyond. It crashed through the tiles, penetrating the somewhat rotten garret-floor and rolled upon the second. The people of the house rushed out in confusion thinking the French had landed, or, that the man on the moon had lost his balance and fallen down. His Grace won the bets, paid all damages, and sent Glenmanna home to his wife Mally with a year's rent in his pocket.

The Duke of Buccleuch, at that time colonel of a regiment of fencibles, happened to be passing between Dumfries and Sanquhar and having made Thornhill his station for the night, he billeted himself on the Duke of Queensberry at Drumlanrig Castle. The latter having enlightened his guest on the characteristics of Glenmanna, it was decided to play a practical joke on the shepherd-Hercules.

Six of the stoutest grenadiers were despatched with orders to go to Glenmanna's quarters, cross him, find fault with everything, quarrel with him, and if possible, overpower and bind him without injuring either his person or his effects. Those were the days (it being towards the end of the 17th century) when roads to Upper Penpont were little better than sheep-tracks. So through moors and mosses, among winding bogs and leaping burns, the redcoats went forward provoking curlews and lapwings, who, to mislead them from their nests, wheeled in airy circuits round them as they made their way past the base of mighty Cairnkinna.

From the top of Glenwhargen they first spied the low-thatched roof of Glenmanna's dwelling, the peat-stack leaning against the gable and a hut – that contrived to pay a triple debt, being barn, byre and stable – attached to the other end of the moor-land sheiling. At a short distance was a round "bucht" in which the shepherd was wont to pen his flock.

The party of militia men arrived at the doorstep a little before noon. Wife Mally was churning butter and had a meal in preparation for her husband, who had not yet returned from "looking his hill". Soldiers were such rare visitors, that had Glenwhargen itself exhibited signs of coming to see them, Mally could scarcely have been more surprised. An uneasy feeling possessed her, as when an "uncanny" bull on entering your garden begins to look narrowly at your flower border when you are on the opposite side. Trying to conceal her uneasiness made her only more awkward, and the soldiers who perceived how timorously she asked them to be seated, began to work upon her fears.

"That bayonet of mine won't clean", said one of the visitors, "since it got soiled with the blood of that confounded old 'herd who dared to refuse us the best that he had". Mally was at this moment dishing the porridge in two wooden bowls for herself and John, when she paused, and letting go the foot of the pot, causing it to fall with such force that it jerked the "cleps" (the iron hooks on which the pot is hung over the fire) out of her hand, and thus pot, porridge and all were dashed upon the floor.

"I'll wipe mine from the old mole's blood before it dries", said the other fellow, "and then it will not rust as yours has done". By this time Mally had reached the threshold.

The porridge first dished was steaming beside those spilt, when one of the soldiers exclaimed, "Hand over that porridge". "Oh, no", retorted Mally, "if there's ae thing on earth our gudeman Jock would go through fire and water for – it's his porridge cog. If he met his best friend in the middle of his porridge, he wouldna let on he kenned him", said she, making a desperate attempt to take the humorous view of the situation. "But, gude friends, I assure you, he'll brain you if you do that", she again exclaimed as the stranger clutched the dish sacred to her lord, while at the same time she swept a cupboard of its bread and butter with a view to serving them. Despite that, nothing would satisfy her remorseless guests except that each should have a spoon to eat that porridge

Enter Glenmanna: "What's a' this, and wha's a' this?" "Well, sir, the Duke of Queensberry says it's alright for us to stay with you", replied one of the redcoats. Glenmanna replied: "You're mair free than welcome, I doot. A nicht's lodging ye'll get since sent frae the Duke, but did the Duke say ye're to yoke on my porridge like a wheen collies?"

"Like what?" replied one of the redcoats, "Hold your peace, you clodpole, we are the king's servants and ought to be served without a grumble". "Go", interrupted the leader, "put a bullet through that fine fat calf and let's be jolly with a roast on the moors, if old clodhopper's wife can cook it. Come Mrs Braxy, take your mouth from your master's ear and attend", for Mally was whispering to Glenmanna in an attempt to calm him down. Instead, her whispering had quite a different effect from that intended, to the joy of the soldiers, who saw the tempest rising.

"Ye'll roast my calf – I'll roast you", exclaimed the shepherd. "Down with him, down with him", roared the soldiers. Glenmanna had only time to toss his plaid on the bed and throw down his staff that was too long for fighting at close quarters. Turning round like a stag at bay he seized the first fellow by the collar and the thigh, and using him both as his sword and shield with such force and fury, that, glad to find the way to the door, the opposing party got outside more terrified than injured. The one that was trussed in Glenmanna's embrace was bruised black and blue. Feeling him self becoming the consistency of jelly, he howled most piteously for mercy, but Glenmanna was deaf to his cries. He rushed outside with him, but spying a cart placed on end, he tossed the soldier onto the grass and tore one of its shafts off. Then, armed with that huge wooden limb over his shoulder, he set off in the track of his enemies.

Glenmanna set off in the track of his enemies

A chase now took place with none to match it in the annals of Penpont or Durisdeer. The soldiers were the quickest, while their pursuer had the longest wind. The heels of the soldiers were spurred with fear, while those of Glenmanna were winged with rage. At the top of Glenwhargen, the five, somewhat scattered, looked back, but they seemed not to have gained a yard. At Cairnkinna, favoured by his knowledge of the ground, the shepherd was no farther from the last one than the length of his evening shadow.

At Gowkthorn they daren't look round – they heard the "thud" of the strongman's footsteps and the wheezing of his throat. Fortunately for them that was when Glenmanna fell. He was up in a minute, but as the ground slopes towards Drumlanrig the soldiers gained so much that from then on, hope became a motive for their speed.

Staggering like men overcome with drink they reached the western staircase that leads into the court of the castle. Informed by the servants of their approach, the two Dukes were waiting to receive them behind the balustrade. The poor fellows had to be wiped of dust and sweat, and restored by stimulants. Glenmanna rushed up only three minutes behind. The cart shaft was on his shoulders and his lips were covered with foam like the winner of the Derby.

The Duke of Queensberry, though used to turning the helm of Glenmanna whichever way he pleased, hadn't the heart to meet him in this mood and left the first brunt of the encounter to the Duke of Buccleuch. He however, failed to stop him, for Glenmanna rushed past upstairs into the court of the castle. Confronted by a number of doors he became confused and made for the kitchen, the road to which he knew best. Here he found a cook, fat and good-natured as Falstaff, and various servants with happy faces and soft words. One offered him spirits and water, another put forward a chair, while the cook herself took the cart shaft as a handy bit of future fuel. These all helped to calm him down and restore the shepherd's long-lost calm composure.

"Hang it", he exclaimed after a deep pause, "it's been a' a trick o' the Duke's after a'. I see through it. I see it a'. Dangerous though, richt dangerous! I micht hae choked aff the first ane like a curlew, or mauled the neist one like a rat". There then followed an explanation of the bet between the two Dukes and a session of handshaking and apologies.

Mally, with a woman's forgiveness had cared for the bruised soldier left on the grass. When Glenmanna got home, the king's servant, well wrapped up in blankets, was able to be placed on horseback behind a guide and conducted safely to Drumlanrig.

Glenmanna died in 1705 after a long life. It is sad to think that his death was the result of over-exertion in lifting an immense stone.

Chapter 6
Old "Q"

While James the Duke of Queensberry clearly enjoyed a wager, nothing surpassed William, the last Duke of Queensberry (1725-1810), or old "Q" as he was called. He inherited the title when James' direct line of succession eventually died out. The delight that William took in both winning money, and proving his cleverness, also aroused in him a love of breaking records. It pleased him to be told that such and such a thing could not be done, and then to prove that it could. One of his most celebrated wagers was to demonstrate how fast a man could travel in a wheeled vehicle.

Coaches and post-chaises lumbered along the badly constructed roads of the period at only a few miles an hour. A gentleman's carriage, drawn by fast horses, could travel at about ten miles an hour. Young William Douglas, examining the problem in detail, announced one day that he could produce a four-wheeled carriage, drawn by four horses, which could carry a man nineteen miles in one hour.

The claim was thought ridiculous. Nothing like that speed had ever been achieved before, and when William showed his willingness to back his claim with hard cash, some heavy bets were at once entered in his betting book. The main bet was with a certain Theobald Taaffe, known also as Count Taaffe, and Andrew Sprowle, and it was for a thousand guineas – a very large sum for a young Scots peer of seemingly moderate means (this was when he was still the Earl of March and before he inherited the Queensberry title in 1778). However, William Douglas shared the bet with one of his old cronies, the Earl of Eglington, who also helped him with his plans. Taaffe, who had once been an MP was a wild Irishman, noted gambler and very near to being a crook. William's associate Lord Eglington was also something of a ne'er do well. No one concerned in the wager was a fool.

Numerous side bets were struck over the event and William began to make his plans with his accustomed thoroughness.

In those days the techniques of carriage building were still surprisingly undeveloped. A gentleman's carriage might well be ornately fitted and lavishly decorated, but mechanically it was usually an indifferent piece of work. Little had been discovered about springing and nothing at all about pneumatic tyres. English coachbuilders produced heavy and cumbersome vehicles which were immensely strong and stood up well to the violent treatment they received on the bad roads of the period, but they were not very fast.

William Douglas approached one of the best and least conservative craftsmen, Wright of Long Acre, and set him to work designing a coach on completely original lines. The terms of the wager were that the vehicle should "carry a man", but they did not state that he had to be carried in a carriage as such. William decided that a body was therefore unnecessary. All that were required were four wheels joined by the lightest possible framework.

Weight, in fact, was the crux of the whole matter and every ounce that could be dispensed with was sacrificed. What Wright finally produced was really no more than two sets of wheels joined by a central bar, which was of thinnest wood bound with wire. The driver was slung on leather straps between the two back wheels, on a tiny seat covered with velvet. The harness, usually a fairly weighty item in carriage equipment, was in this case constructed out of whale-bone and silk. Silk was also used for the traces. Thus weight was reduced as far as possible, while strength was still preserved, for the vehicle had to cover nineteen miles on a far from even surface.

The terms of the wager did not state a carriage as such

After being tested and found satisfactory, the vehicle was weighed. The total weight of carriage and harness was two and a half hundredweight (about 125kgs).

The next problem was the selection and training of the horses. Fortunately for William Douglas and his partner the terms of the wager gave them ample time to carry out their tests – but they had to give two months notice of the date of the match.

The best horses were obtained and rigorously trained. So rigorously, indeed, that seven of them died under the trials of the severity to which they were subjected. This was a matter of no consequence to William, to whom horseflesh was always expendable, but their defection caused him much additional expense. Finally he was able to assemble a team of four he considered strong enough and fast enough (three in fact were ex-racehorses). Trained reserves were also available in case of any last-minute accident. Each of the four horses carried a rider on its back, whilst the driver, or "passenger", carried William's colours of red and black. The riders, or postilions as they really were, wore blue satin waist coats, buckskin breeches, white silk stockings and black velvet caps, for William Douglas was nothing if not a showman.

The day fixed for the event was 29 August 1750. The time seven o'clock in the morning. The place was Newmarket heath. The course was via the Warren and Rubbing Houses, through the ditch – the gap in the ancient mound known as the Devil's Dyke that runs north and south across the Heath – then to the right, three times round a staked piece of ground of four miles and then back to the starting point.

A large crowd gathered to watch the event and wagering on the outcome continued while the final preparations were being made. A well-known Newmarket character called Tuting was appointed an official course-clearer and he led the parade wearing a jacket of crimson velvet. Three umpires had been appointed. Armed with stop watches, they took up different positions to ensure that there was no cheating – a necessary precaution when the gamesters involved were known to be so astute.

William Douglas had no doubt about the outcome. His plans had been carefully made and he knew that only an unforeseen accident could prevent him from winning his wager. His riders were told to hold a little in reserve, so that the match could be kept alive and betting would continue while the race was being run.

As it happened, the only thing that went wrong was that the horses, trained to the peak of fitness and eager to go, set off at such a pace that they could not be restrained and covered the first four miles in nine minutes, thus achieving a speed of over 26 miles an hour. Thus Taaffe and Sprowle knew that they had lost their wager before a quarter of the course had been covered and the betting was brought to a standstill. The full distance of nineteen miles was covered in 53 minutes and 27 seconds.

The result did far more than win William Douglas a handsome wager. It established his reputation in Mayfair as an outstanding sportsman and a king amongst gamblers, even though he was not yet 25. When he returned to London from Newmarket, he was welcomed as a hero and accepted as a leader of the fast set. Now everyone knew him and all sportsmen admired and respected him. He was delighted. He probably made very little out of the event, because his expenses were so heavy, but in this instance he knew that the money had been well spent. His reputation was made.

On another occasion he claimed that he would send a message a distance of 50 miles in one hour. His opponents were becoming wary of his ingenuity, but this claim seemed impossible. No man had ever achieved such a speed, unless it were a tobogganist flying down a steep hill over hard snow, and so the bets were struck and everyone waited to see what new trick William Douglas was about to pull out of the hat.

In this case his ingenuity was not greatly taxed. He merely assembled a team of twenty cricketers, each an adept at catching and throwing, and placed them in a wide circle. The letter was then enclosed in a cricket ball, which the cricketers flung from one to the other. So long as no catches were dropped – and none was – the task was comparatively easy. The ball travelled repeatedly round the circle and the letter travelled the 50 miles in under the hour.

Old Q was the last of the Douglases of Drumlanrig. He had no sons or male Douglas heirs and knew that upon his death the dukedom, with the greater portion of the estates, would pass to the Duke of Buccleuch. He had an intense hatred for the Scotts and to spite his noble successor he did all in his power to diminish the value of the property after his own death, and maliciously denuded the braes of Nithsdale of their grand old trees. He altered the system of the farm leases, and in consideration of a certain lump sum paid as "entry money", he granted, at incredibly low rentals, fresh leases of nineteen years duration, that were renewed each year so as to ensure as heavy a loss as possible to Buccleuch.

Some years after the succession of the Scotts, which was in 1810, arrangements were made for terminating the leases granted by Old Q, and large sums were paid to the tenants for their surrender. This "breaking of the tacks" was the making of many of the farmers, for it gave them capital in hand that enabled them to purchase stock and improve their holdings.

Chapter 7
Tales of the Covenanters

Upper Nithsdale, with its wood-covered glens, moors and lonely hillsides was for years the retreats and hiding places of the persecuted Covenanters.

The martyr's graves, scattered here and there in the district, are silent but impressive witnesses of the part it shared in what has appropriately been called "The Killing Times".

It all began when the Dean of St. Giles' Kirk in Edinburgh tried to introduce Charles the First's Book of Common Prayer on 23 July 1637. An old vegetable seller called Jenny Geddes showed her resentment by throwing her stool at the Dean's head, declaring that she wasn't going to participate in "Papery". Her public act of disgust was followed by the rest of the congregation and soon spread throughout Scotland.

King Charles the First was a monarch who belonged to a dynasty that had several members who were tyrants. He himself was a bigoted puppet of Rome who had no sympathy, but rather a supreme contempt for the religious liberties which the Scottish people claimed as a natural right. He went on to fall out with his parliament in Westminster, started a civil war and was finally defeated by Cromwell's army and beheaded.

The Sanquhar Declarations of 1680 and 1685 commemorated by the monument in Sanquhar High Street are generally considered to have sounded the death knell of the Stuart Dynasty.

Richard Cameron, known as "The Lion of the Covenant" and his brother Michael chose the Burgh of Sanquhar to publicly declare a momentous manifesto, the "Sanquhar Declaration". On 22 June 1680, the brothers, accompanied by twenty horsemen, rode down the High Street, and after praise and prayer. Michael read and afterwards affixed the Declaration to the Mercat Cross, as it was then known. Although there were in fact six Declarations, undoubtedly the most famous was the one by Cameron and this left a mark on the country's history.

Cameron and his comrades rode out of the Burgh as sedately and unmolested as they had entered it. They took to the hills and moors of Dumfriesshire and Ayrshire. The Government immediately became

The Covenanters fought valiantly and desperately

alarmed and military search parties were sent out. At the same time a proclamation was issued, naming those who had accompanied Cameron to Sanquhar and offering rewards for their capture, dead or alive.

At the end of four weeks, on the afternoon of 20 July, at Airdsmoss, a morass between Cumnock and Muirkirk, Cameron and his devoted companions, 63 in all, were surrounded by dragoons under the command of Bruce of Earlshall. The contest that ensued was fierce, a thunderstorm at the time added to the fearfulness of the fighting. The Covenanters fought valiantly and desperately. While only nine of them, including Cameron, were killed, it was said that twenty-eight of their opponents were slain.

An immediate effect of the Sanquhar Declaration was the extremely rigorous measures adopted by the authorities for the apprehension of the "Cameronians" and all known frequenters of conventicles (illegal gatherings in the open air for worship). A strong military force was sent into Lanarkshire, Nithsdale and Galloway, with strict orders to search for, arrest, and if need be, put to instant death, all persons who, upon oath, refused to disown the Declaration.

No government of course could have tolerated the treasonable proceedings of the Cameronians – but the severities inflicted upon them and other Covenanters far exceeded the measure of their offence. It was persecution, and this period has been well named "The Killing Times". From now onward, for the next eight years, Upper Nithsdale was almost entirely dominated by the military.

There is scarcely a place in Upper Nithsdale that is not associated with the persecution of the Covenanters. The whole of Upper Nithsdale was traversed by Covenanters seeking concealment and rest in its wild and lonely places, and time and again the glens and moor-lands re-echoed the trampling of the dragoons and the shots that sent many a hapless "rebel" to his grave.

Upper Nithsdale was ideal terrain for Covenanters to hide out and evade capture by the dragoons. They were helped by many brave folk who discreetly afforded them food, shelter or information. Typical is the tale of a Covenanter sympathiser who lived on Eliock Muir that overlooks Sanquhar. She was a "venerable matron", whose house was an occasional resort to the wandering Covenanters who lived among the wild hills and glens in the area. A soldier belonging to the company that were garrisoned at Eliock often visited her lonely house by stealth – conveyed secret information with regard to the movement of the troopers, so that her friends in hiding might look to themselves and pass on the warning to their brethren in other places.

It was also said that a domestic servant in Eliock House used to overhear his masters discussing their plans in the parlour and then place himself under the awning of a wide-spreading tree and tell the tree the secret that he wished to convey. Meanwhile, in a cavity in its fantastic roots lay someone who listened to his words and then instantly carried the tidings to the suffering brethren who availed themselves of the warning.

Not far from there on the farm of South Mains, opposite the town of Sanquhar, lived William Hair, who was in the habit of concealing the wanderers about his house. On one occasion he had a few of them in his barn when some of the troopers from Eliock arrived at his door. As he dreaded that they had come to search the premises he was very concerned for the safety of those he was hiding. To his pleasant surprise, however, he found they had come to obtain corn for their horses, which they wished to purchase from him.

He led them into the barn to examine the heaps on the floor which alarmed those who were hidden among the straw at the thought of having the enemy so near to them. It would only have taken the accidental removal of a little of the straw, or sheaves of corn to reveal them. You can imagine their relief when the party peacefully left the place without ever knowing how close they were to the fugitives.

About the commencement of the persecution in Scotland, nearly three hundred and fifty ministers were ejected from their churches, in the severity of winter, and driven to seek shelter among the peasants. These ministers were forbidden to preach, even in the fields, or to approach within twenty miles of their former charges.

Often in the lonely moor-lands, out of sight of the vigilant eyes of their persecutors, these outcasts continued to preach at illegal conventicles. One of the most renowned of these worthies who persisted in preaching the gospel in the wilds of his native land, at the constant risk of death, was the venerable Peden. He had no home, and so spent much of his time in the fields. The caves by the hill stream, the dense hazel wood in the deep glen, the feathery brackens on the hill, the green corn when it was tall enough to conceal him, afforded him by turns, when necessary, a hiding place from his pursuers.

Among the many hiding places to which this man occasionally retreated, was the solitude of Glendyne, about three miles to the east of Sanquhar. A better hiding place than this is rarely to be found. Glendyne stretches eastward, winding among the hills for nearly three miles. The width of the glen at the bottom is in many places little more than five or six times the width of the burn that rushes through it. Dark precipitous hills, frowning on either side, rise from the level of the valley to a great height. Near the lower end of the glen – which in ancient times was thickly covered with trees – and where it ends its sinuous journey's course with one majestic sweep, reaching forward to the bleak moor-lands beneath, the revered worthy had selected for himself a place of refuge.

On one occasion, he ventured forth from this lair to visit nearby Auchentaggart Farm where a known sympathiser lived. While enjoying refreshments and the company of other wanderers in this house, a company of soldiers appeared at the door. The poor men within saw that there was little likelihood of escape, and together suddenly rushed out through the door, scared the horses, stupefied the troopers and fled in the direction of Glendyne, whose steep banks prevented a successful pursuit, and in this way escaped.

As Peden fled across the moor, and about to pass a burn, he spotted a cavity underneath its bank that had been scooped out by the running water. Into this he instinctively crept, and stretching himself at full length, lay hidden. In a short while, the dragoons came on, and having followed close in his track, reached the very spot where he was hiding. As the heavy horses came thundering over the turf on the edge of the burn, the foot of one of them sank through the sod, grazed his head and pressed his bonnet into the soft clay, while he escaped unhurt.

Then there is the nearly tragic consequence of a confusion of identity between Adam Clark of Glenim and the son of his relative, Andrew Clark of neighbouring Auchengruith Farm that also neighbours Auchentaggart and Glendyne.

Adam Clark was a well-known Covenanter, who had many scrapes with the dragoons. On one occasion, a company of troopers who were on their way to the wilds of Crawford Moor, for the purpose of surprising a conventicle, called at Glenim, which lay directly in their route, to ask for a guide to conduct them over the heights. When the party drew up before the door, Adam Clark went out to meet them. The story goes that, being roused from his bed in the dark of early morning, he was stooping to draw one of his shoes more firmly on his foot when he was jostled by one of the horses and nearly knocked down. In recovering his position, he lost his temper and struck the animal a furious blow on the face which made it retreat rather hastily and awkwardly for its rider. The dragoon instantly presented a pistol to Clark's breast with the apparent intention of shooting him on the spot.

The commander of the party saw the mischief that might befall and intervened by presenting the broadside of his sword to the dragoon. He prevented him from fulfilling his purpose and proceeded to declare that they had come with no hostile intent, but simply to request the assistance of a guide.

This event probably took place near the beginning of the persecution before the loyalties of the Clarks, both of Auchengruith and Glenim, became widely known. When order was restored and both parties had come to a better understanding, Clark consented to conduct them across the wilds.

When they came to the Stake Moss on the west side of the Lowther Hills, not far from Wanlockhead, it occurred to Clark that it was now in his power to cause some inconvenience that might possibly slow their progress and prevent them from accomplishing their intended mischief.

This moss presents an irregular surface, with here and there deep hags and some marshy springs. In the moor-land districts in the south-west of Scotland, some of these springs, or cold wells as the shepherds used to call them, are of great depth, reaching occasionally from six to twelve feet, and in some cases to a much greater depth. Their width is sometimes about two or three feet, and their length sometimes double that. The water in these wells rises to a level with the surrounding heath and their surface is generally covered with long grass and aquatic weeds. A dragoon stumbling into one of these larger wells would inevitably perish, and this accounts for the tradition respecting the occasional and entire disappearance of some of the troopers, man and horse, in the moors.

It was in the dusk of the early morning when the party arrived at the Stake Moss, and the bad light was favourable to Clark's plan. They had followed him in safety for several miles and, not being suspicious of their guide, were riding behind him in perfect confidence.

When they reached the morass, Clark, being on foot, pressed forward, leaping the mossy ditches with nimble bounds and left the horses behind, plunging one after another into the sinking peat and getting stuck fast. When Clark saw that the party were fully mired and that there was little chance of getting free for a considerable time, he made his escape over the dark heath and left them to help themselves.

Clark left the horses mired in the sinking peat

It was said that he often regretted his conduct on this occasion, both because the commander of the party had treated him honourably and because it would tend to exasperate the enemy and subject all his friends throughout the district to still more rigorous treatment. His suspicions weren't groundless. The more injury the Covenanters inflicted on their opponents in self-defence, the more severe did their own sufferings become afterwards, for their enemies delighted in nothing more than the opportunity of retaliating with sevenfold vengeance. It appears that Adam Clark, from the time that he led the troopers into the moss was regarded as a dangerous man and one whom, on the first opportunity they were determined to apprehend. This determination was amply manifested in the following tragic scene that was nearly fully acted out on the bent grass in front of the house of Auchengruith.

It appears that one of the other Adam Clark of Auchenguith sons, also called Andrew, bore a striking resemblance to his cousin, Adam Clark of Glenim. One day, the dragoons met Andrew on the moors and, believing him to be the same person who had guided them into the moss, apprehended him and took him to his father's house. The commander of the party is said to have been Colonel James Douglas who had been granted an ample commission with a judicial power for the purpose of harassing the south and the west.

The poor captive was interrogated about his beliefs and especially with respect to his conduct at the moss. He declared that he was not the person to whom they alluded and that, however a strong resemblance there might be between him and the individual who had done them the injury of which they complained, he was entirely innocent. The soldiers, however, positively affirmed that he was the very man, who, in the grey of the morning, conducted them along the heights and left them in the morass. There, they asserted, they had lost some of their best horses after breaking their legs in the moss.

In those days the execution of a man after his impeachment was but the work of a moment. Andrew was immediately taken to the field in front of the house to be instantly shot. He was allowed time to pray – a favour which in similar circumstances was not granted to everyone. He knelt down on the bent and in the presence of his enemies and his father's household, he prayed.

The supplications of this good man produced a deep impression on the dragoons who stood around guarding him. One of the party, more hardened than the rest, perceiving the effect it was having on his fellow dragoons, commanded him to rise from his knees. "No", said the leader, "let the poor man continue in his prayer, we can afford to wait a while as other matters are not pressing. Give the man leisure as his time on earth is but short".

There are few hearts so hardened as to outbrave a scene of this nature without some emotion. James Douglas, though he had witnessed many an act of cruelty, was in the present instance, scarcely immune from the moving spectacle of a fellow man uttering his last prayer in the presence

"Halt, soldiers", she cried,
raising her staff with authority

of weeping and agonising friends. He probably now wanted only a slight pretext to set the poor victim free and that pretext was soon found.

There lived in the neighbourhood, at a place called Howats Burnfoot, a worthy old woman who had been Andrew Clark's nurse and for whom, as is common in such cases, she cherished a more than ordinary affection. To this good woman's house a messenger had been instantly despatched to convey the information of what was going on at Auchengruith. She was a tough old woman who had accompanied her husband for sixteen years in the continental wars and had experienced a variety of fortune.

It was said that on one occasion, at the storming of a certain town, her husband had been severely wounded. She first rendered him what assistance was necessary and then grasped his sword and pressed forward with the assailants to the attack. This woman lost no time in presenting herself before Colonel Douglas and his company. The sight of soldiers, even in their most terrific array, did not frighten her, for she was familiar with war.

When she arrived at the scene of distress, Andrew had ended his prayer and the soldiers were prepared and waiting their commander's orders to pour the contents of their muskets into the body of the innocent victim. "Halt, soldiers", cried the matron, whose venerable and commanding appearance inspired the party with something like awe. "Halt, soldiers", she cried, raising her staff with authority as generals are accustomed to do with the naked blade of their swords on the battlefield, "halt, and then listen to me. Let not the brown heath on the moors of Auchengruith be stained with the blood of an innocent man, lest it cry for vengeance in a voice so loud as not to be denied".

"How now, good mother", said Douglas. "What have you to offer in defence of this rebel who has done what he could to damage his Majesty's interests? You have heard of the affair at Stake Moss?"

The old woman replied, "I have, but hear me. This man is not the one you have to blame for that affair. He may be like him – he may be his very picture, but he is not the same. The person who did that deed is not for me to say, nor shall I. But sire, if you are a true soldier, listen to the wife of one who warred under the banner of your honoured uncle in countries far from this. For your uncle's sake, by whose side my husband fought and bled, and for whose sake he would have sacrificed his life, I beg the life of this man. I beg on my knees for the life of this innocent man". "My good woman", replied the colonel, "his life you shall have. Your appearance is the guarantee for the truth of your statements and you have mentioned a name that has weight with me. Soldiers! Let him go!"

In this way was the tragic scene at Auchengruith ended and Andrew Clark restored to the arms of his rejoicing friends.

These are just some of the tales of narrow escapes by Covenanters in the area, but not all were so lucky. As stated earlier, Upper Nithsdale has many graves filled by the martyrs who were executed where they stood and I will relate some of their tales in the next chapter.

Chapter 8
The Killing Times and the death of the Laird of Lag

The cruel persecution of the Covenanters is typified by the story of the martyrdom of William Smith. He seems to have been assisting his father who farmed at Hill, a mile to the east of Moniaive, and was in the fields when he was met by Cornet Bailie. The usual questions were put to him by the Cornet, but when Smith declined to answer them he was taken to Caitloch, a house a mile to the north-west of Moniaive and where a garrison was stationed.

Tidings of his son's capture were brought to the father, who waited on his laird, Sir Robert Laurie of Maxwelton, to use his influence on his son's behalf. Sir Robert had a daughter married that day and the father had doubtless thought that the fact of the marriage would be in his favour. Sir Robert Laurie was prevailed upon to meet Cornet Bailie next day at Glencairn Kirk, but it was with no intention, as the meeting showed, to accede to the father's desire.

On the appointed hour of 3 March 1685, William Smith was brought before them, and when he still refused to answer the ensnaring questions, Sir Robert Laurie, true to his character as an oppressor and persecutor, by virtue of the power he said he had as a commissioner appointed to see the laws against non conformity enforced, passed sentence of death upon him. Cornet Bailie declared such a sentence to be illegal as there had been no "syse" (no trial by jury), but Sir Robert would hear of no delay and threatened to report the Cornet for sparing him so long.

Smith was immediately taken out to the Race Muir, to a large stone in a field to the east of Moniaive, and shot by a party of soldiers. As he prepared to die he declared to the spectators that he died for no rebellion nor for any of the crimes he was charged with. According to him his only crimes were that he had conversed with the persecuted people as they came in his way and that he had refused to disclose where their hiding places were. He also took time to comfort his parents as he bid them farewell.

At the instruction of Sir Robert, his body was refused burial in the churchyard and ordered to be buried under the doorstep of the farmhouse at the Hill. That way his father might be compelled to step over his son's remains and so dishonour them every time he went out, or in to his house. This order was actually carried out and the body lay under the doorstep until the Revolution, when no one will wonder that it was speedily exhumed and buried in the spot where it now lies.

Just as sickening is the story of the execution of five Covenanters who are commemorated on a stone at Ingleston in the parish of Glencairn.

The story of the death of these men is sickening in its brutality. An informer called Andrew Watson, having got wind of their hideout, sold his information to the authorities who immediately despatched Colonel James Douglas and Lieutenant Livingstone to surprise the fugitives. Their cave or "hidie hole" was accordingly surrounded and all of the five made prisoners.

It is said that the soldiers fired a salvo into the cave, wounding one of the fugitives, before rushing in. Without any examination, or the slightest form of trial, Colonel Douglas ordered them to be shot. John Gibson, the one who had been injured was the first to suffer. His sister got in to him by the compassion of some of the soldiers. His mother also managed to get to him and he charged her not to give way to grief, but to bless the Lord upon his account, who had made him both willing and ready to suffer for His cause and interest. After singing part of his favourite psalm and engaging in prayer, he was despatched.

An effort was then made to dispose of the others all at once. The volley killed three of them, while the fourth was left badly wounded but conscious. A renegade dragoon called Ferguson, observing this, drew his sword and thrust it through his body – a fit climax to a tragedy which for cold-blooded cruelty is almost without parallel in Covenanting literature.

Then there is the incident at the "Martyr's Knowe".

In the beginning of the summer of 1685, a year in which the persecution raged fearfully in the south and west, six men from Douglasdale, namely, David Dun, Simon Paterson, John Richard, William Brown, Robert Morris and James Welsh, in their wanderings made their way southward and sought refuge among the more inaccessible heights in the upper parts of Nithsdale.

They concealed themselves in a thicket, in a place called Glenshilloch, a little to the west of Wanlockhead and not far from the ancient farmhouse of Cogshead. This house, now a shepherd's cottage, is situated in a delightful glen and is surrounded by high hills. It was a desirable retreat in those days as there were no regular roads leading to it except solitary footpaths that here and there marked out a track for pedestrians across the hills.

The family who resided at Cogshead at that time was related to William Brown, one of the wanderers who had taken refuge in Glenshilloch. As the two places were near-neighbours, Brown made his way stealthily over the intervening height and informed his friends of the circumstances in which he and his companions in suffering were placed. The sympathy of this household was easily gained and an ample supply of provisions was conveyed to the men in their hiding place.

It is not easy to say how long the party might have continued there among the dense brushwood during the warm days of summer, had not a search been made for then in all the glens and hills in the locality in which it was suspected they had taken refuge.

The report had reached Drumlanrig that a company of refugees from Douglas Water had eluded the pursuit of the dragoons and were concealed somewhere in the wilds between the Mennock and the Crawick. Acting on this information, Drumlanrig collected his troopers for a vigilant search. He formed his party into three divisions, one of which traversed the lonely streams of Mennock, another the pastoral banks of Crawick and the third pursued the middle route by the dark Glendyne. By this means it was confidently expected that the fugitives could not possibly escape, and more especially as no note of warning had been sounded in the district of the persecutors' plans.

The six men who were lying among the hazel bushes, not anticipating any danger in their solitary retreat hadn't taken the precaution of setting guards on the neighbouring hills to give warning of the approach of the enemy.

Drumlanrig himself conducted the middle division of the troopers, and having led them over the hill on the north side of Glendyne, descended on the Water of Cog and took his station on what is now called "The Martyr's Knowe".

It happened that while Drumlanrig and his party were on the hillock, that some of the dragoons who were scouring the adjacent hills in search of the reputed rebels seized a boy who was returning from Glenshilloch to Cogshead carrying an empty wooden vessel. It contained several horn spoons which were proof to the soldiers that he had been carrying provisions to some individuals among the hills and they naturally suspected that those individuals were the very ones they were searching for. Under this impression they took him to their commander, who strictly interrogated him, but without eliciting anything satisfactory.

The firmness of the youth enraged Drumlanrig, who drew his sword with the intention of running him through the body and would have slain him on the spot, had not a second thought occurred that by using other and gentler means he might eventually succeed in obtaining all the information that he desired. With this plan in mind, he had him bound hand and foot, while he sent out the soldiers in the direction in which he had been returning over the hills.

It wasn't long before the troopers, on descending the north side of the hill found the men in their hiding place. They pounced on them as a falcon on its quarry and secured Dun, Paterson and Richard, whilst Brown, Morris and Welsh made their escape. The troopers, having been so far successful in their objective, triumphantly began their return over the hill, but before they reached the rendezvous an unexpected occurrence happened which fairly routed the assailants and accomplished the deliverance of the prisoners.

In hilly districts, when conditions are right at that time of year, sudden thunderstorms can occur. Sometimes the explosions from the clouds and the torrents from the sky are so terrific as to alarm the stoutest of hearts. In these cases the fiery bolts falling incessantly on the hills tear up large areas of the surface of the hill. The tumultuous descent of water, covering the green sides of the hills with white foam, gathers into a torrent that carries moss, soil and rock and scours a trench down the steep slope that later becomes a channel.

It was with one of these sudden storms that Drumlanrig and his party were visited, after gathering unnoticed above them. When the dragoons who had led the three prisoners were within a short distance of Drumlanrig's station on the Martyr's Knowe, the first burst of thunder rattled its startling peal over their heads. The horses snorted and the sheep on the neighbouring heath crowded together as if for mutual protection. The rapid descent of the hail, the loud roaring of the thunder, like the simultaneous discharge of a hundred cannon from the battlement of the hills, and the flashing of the lightning in the faces of the horses, rendered them unmanageable and they bolted in every direction like the fragments of a fleeing army that has been routed on the battlefield.

In the confusion, Drumlanrig himself was panic-struck and fled from the tempest, without thinking of either his men or his prisoners, provided he could obtain a place of shelter. It is not said to what place he fled, but there can be no doubt that it was to the farm of Cogshead, which was scarcely half-a-mile from the place where he stood. When the soldiers saw their master retreating with such haste from the warring of the elements they followed his example and let go the captives. The three men stood undaunted in the storm, and though it was regarded with consternation by their enemies, it was hailed as a friendly deliverer by them, who were constantly exposed to the pitiless storms of a wretched persecution, compared to which the fierce raging of the elements was mildness itself.

When the prisoners found themselves at liberty and shrouded in the mantle of the murky tempest, they resolved to embrace the opportunity

Drumlanrig himself fled from the tempest

of instant flight. As they passed the Martyr's Knowe, they observed someone lying on the summit, apparently lifeless. This they found to be the little boy who had brought them provisions in the morning and whom Drumlanrig, in his haste, had left bound on the spot. They untied him and found that he wasn't dead but only stunned with terror. Having raised him up and informed him of what had occurred they told him to keep himself hidden till the soldiers had left the glen. They then went westward and sought a retreat among the wilds in the upper parts of Galloway.

The other three who escaped at Glenshilloch, namely Brown, Morris and Welsh, fled northward but were intercepted by the party who were sent to the Crawick valley. Brown and Morris were shot at the back of Craignorth, where they lie buried at the places where they respectively fell at Brown Cleuch and Morris Cleuch. Welsh, however, managed to escape and remained in hiding among the Nithsdale hills.

King Charles the Second's chief agents in southern Scotland were that trinity of destroyers – William (1637-1695), third Earl of Queensberry, Justice General, Lord Drumlanrig (1662-1711), his son, and Colonel John Graham of Claverhouse and Claypots (1649-1689) and their local abetters, Grierson of Lag, Douglas of Morton, Dalyell of Glenae, and others.

Sir Robert Grierson of Lag Tower in Dunscore, or the "Laird of Lag" as he was known locally, was considered by many to be one of the cruellest persecutors of Covenanters in Nithsdale. The popular account of Lag's last illness and burial are exceedingly grotesque.

During the latter part of his life, Sir Robert had taken up his abode in his town lodgings in Dumfries. It was an ancient pile of a building of singular construction, facing the principal part of the High Street of the town, then known as the "Plainstones". This old house was called the "Turnpike" from the spiral staircase, a characteristic of it, as of many of the old Edinburgh houses. It was situated at the head of what was called Turnpike Close, and little more than two hundred yards from the River Nith.

The best known of the many legends regarding Lag is that when he came near his end, and was sorely tormented with gout, he had relays of servants posted so as to hand up from one to another a succession of buckets of cold water from the Nith, that he might cool his burning limbs – but the moment his feet were inserted into the water, it began to fizz and boil.

Sir Robert died in this old Turnpike house on 31 December 1733. He had grown so corpulent in his latter days that his body could not be decently carried down the winding stair for burial. Accordingly, a portion of the wall between two windows looking onto the Plainstones had to be temporarily removed, and through the wide hole thus created the coffin was lowered down. The building was eventually demolished in 1826, but the incident is commemorated by the nearby public house called "The Hole i' the Wall Inn".

It was said that a "corbie" (carrion crow) perched itself on the coffin and would not be driven off, but accompanied the funeral cortege to the grave in the churchyard of Dunscore.

Moreover, when the funeral procession started and had only gone a short distance, it was found that the horses, with all their struggles and dripping with perspiration from some mysterious cause could move the hearse no further. Sir Thomas Kirkpatrick of Closeburn, the old friend and comrade of Lag (and his relative), who was believed to be deep in some branch of the Black Art, was one of the mourners. On this occasion he swore a great oath that he would drive the hearse of Lag "though the Devil was in it". He ordered a team of beautiful Spanish horses of his own to be harnessed in the place of the others. Sir Thomas mounted and took the reins, when the horses instantly dashed off at a furious gallop that he couldn't restrain, and they never eased up their headlong pace till they reached the Dunscore churchyard, where they suddenly pulled up – and died.

There have been few occasions of rarer jollity than that of old Lag's funeral. With the last of the year of 1733, his chequered life went out and straightway there set in a course of feasting and a flow of drink that apparently had begun before the man was dead and carried on during the first fortnight of the New Year. Much wine was consumed before the burial and a good supply was sent out for consumption at the churchyard.

Thus the legends regarding Lag, who made his name a terror, even after he was dead, were handed down and remain until this day.

One of the few victories for the Covenanters over the military took place in the foreground of this view, just above where Glen Valentine enters from the right. On the Tuesday 29 July, 1684 a party of dragoons was escorting prisoners to be lodged in Edinburgh prior to exile as slaves to Carolina, when they were ambushed in this narrow defile by about sixteen rescuers. The dragoon Sergeant Kelt was shot dead and the rescue effected, although the eventual capture and execution of six of the rescuers on August 15th marked the beginning of the "Killing Times". A line of telegraph poles marching up the glen now removes a little of the atmosphere of brooding desolation.

Chapter 9
Tales involving horses in Upper Nithsdale

Sanquhar is rightly proud of having the oldest working post office in the world. Post offices are a development of the old Mongol system of relaying messages quickly by riders on horseback who changed mounts at regular stages, or staging posts.

Stagecoaches had begun running between England and Scotland, and afterwards between certain towns in Scotland, as early as the middle of the seventeenth century. The journey to London took many days while it took the best part of a week to travel from York to that city. The delay was largely due to the poor roads and it was noted in 1685 as a great feat that the Duke of Queensberry and other noblemen had travelled from London to Edinburgh in eight days.

There were no regular services of stagecoaches, however, on the Nithsdale road till 100 years later. In the early years of the 19th century there was a daily service. One coach owned by Major Logan, of Knockenstob, and others, was called "The Independent" and put up at the Queensberry Inn on Sanquhar's High Street, while another was named "The Burns", and at a later period a third, called the "Times" was added. A keen rivalry sprang up between them, and racing was a daily occurrence, affording a great deal of amusement to the townsfolk. The Burns was withdrawn but The Independent continued to run till the opening of the railway.

The arrival of the coach was the principal event of the day. The toot of the guard's horn, the crack of the driver's whip, and the gaily painted coach as it dashed up the street, drawn by its team of four steaming horses, roused the sleepy towns. The townsfolk of Sanquhar peeped out of doors, or hurried to the inn to learn the news, while the youngsters crowded around, their highest ambition being to walk one of the horses round the stable yard till it had cooled, and then to ride it bareback to the River Nith for a wash. Indeed, that simple task was often the first lesson many a young lad had in the equestrian art.

In Thornhill the stagecoach horses were staged at the Buccleuch Inn and the Thornhill Inn before carrying on to Edinburgh.

The Bow Entry, West Morton Street, Thornhill, provided access to the rear of the
Thornhill Inn, and was built in 1851. Some of the oldest single storey cottages in
Thornhill remained behind this entry until it was demolished in the 1960's
to provide the access needed for the building of St Cuthbert's Walk.

Durisdeer. The church is the burial place of the Dukes of Buccleuch and is famous
for the Queensberry Marbles. This view shows one of the old stone bings at the
side of the road. The farmers carted the stones from their fields, then the
stone-nappers broke them up and they were used to make the roads.

On one occasion the Carlisle to Edinburgh coach was snowed up at Durisdeer Mill. It was a tremendous storm lasting three days and all communication between the hamlet and the outer world was cut off. The passengers were hospitably entertained, but such an unexpected increase in the little population shortened their supply of provisions to the point where they began to think that they were going to run out and suffer from hunger. A young serving maid, on looking into one of the passengers' bedrooms saw him brushing his teeth. Evidently this was something that she was not familiar with, for she ran down the lobby crying, "Oh, Mistress, we're done for noo. The gentlemen are beginning to sharpen their teeth wi' a wee white file".

The opening of the railway dealt the fatal blow to the coach system, and so one of the most picturesque features of the social life of our small country towns disappeared.

As already said, the mail was carried on horseback and latterly by mail gigs. They were privately owned, and besides the Government subsidy, a good deal was earned by carrying small parcels and sometimes a stray passenger or two.

The direct road from Sanquhar to Glasgow on foot by Muirkirk and Strathaven was shorter than that taken by the coach via Kilmarnock, the former being about 48 miles and the latter about 58 miles. William Cunningham, a watchmaker in Sanquhar, laid a bet that he would cover the distance between the two places in less time than the coach.

Cunningham was a powerfully built man who walked with a big swinging step. They started, both the coach and he, from the Tron steeple in Glasgow, and when the coach swept round the turn of the road at the Council House

The driver was astonished to see
Cunningham standing at the Inn's close

in Sanquhar, the driver was astonished to see Cunningham standing at the inn's close awaiting its arrival to claim payment of the bet. Running at an average speed of six miles an hour he had done the journey in eight hours, and won with twenty minutes to spare.

Another great equestrian tale from Sanquhar involved the impounding of a valuable horse in 1888. It belonged to "Lord" George Sanger, the well-known circus proprietor of the time, and was taken as security for custom dues, an event that at the time caused great excitement.

Under powers granted by the Royal Charter, the Town Council had for close on three centuries levied a toll upon all animals, carriages and goods entering or passing through the burgh. These tolls, known as custom dues, were for many years the principal source of the town revenue.

On many occasions travelling showmen had objected to paying the custom and stormy scenes frequently ensued.

On one memorable Sunday, in the early 1870s, a circus proprietor, who refused to pay, struck out with his whip at the burgh officer and attempted to proceed through the town without paying. It would have been better for him if he had paid the demand quietly. The townsfolk were angry at

"Lord" George Sanger's Circus passed through Sanquhar

the assault on their officer and in retaliation made an attack upon the showman's gorgeously decorated caravans. They smashed the mirrors and gilding, and would have soon wrecked everything had the showman not relented and paid the money due. The damage to the caravans cost a lot of money to repair.

The Roads and Bridges Act that came into force in 1887 abolished the right to levy custom on traffic through the burgh. Unfortunately the Town Council hadn't properly understood the Act and the burgh officer continued to collect the dues as before.

On Sunday 8 July 1888, shortly after noon, "Lord" George Sanger's mammoth circus passed through Sanquhar on its journey from Cumnock to Dumfries. Preceded by the band carriage, "Lord" George, in a pony and trap, headed a long procession of caravans and wagons, elephants and camels, and troops of horses.

On entering the burgh he was stopped by James Stoddart, the burgh officer, who demanded payment of the custom dues. "Lord" George flatly, but politely enough, refused to make any payment and asserted that the burgh no longer had the right to levy any such charge. To avoid any delay or disturbance, he invited the officer to take a horse, or a dozen if he liked, as security for payment of the dues should it be found, on trial in a court of law, that they were due to be paid.

Stoddart, thinking it was an easy way out of a difficulty, accordingly took possession of a fine thoroughbred horse, and "Lord" George and his retinue passed on their way. The impounded horse was stabled at the Queensberry Inn.

Next day, Provost Fingland went to Dumfries and took counsel, with the result that a petition was lodged with the Sheriff Clark on behalf of the magistrates for authority to sell the horse to meet their claim. The same day Sanger's legal adviser came to Sanquhar demanding delivery of the thoroughbred and offering to deposit £10 in lieu of it until settlement of the action. This demand was at first refused. The following day, having had time to consider their position, the magistrates withdrew their petition for power to sell and sent the horse on to "Lord" George who was in Carlisle by then. His "Lordship" then began an action of damages for the horse's detention.

Provost Fingland was forced to admit that a mistake had been made and began negotiations to settle the matter as best he could for the burgh. Finally, an out-of-court settlement of the case was agreed and the Town Council paid "Lord" George £50 damages for detention of his horse – a performing animal that was a considerable feature of the show – as well as all of the expenses that he had occurred in connection with the action. Altogether the seizure of Sanger's horse cost the burgh the sum of £68 4s 5d. That was a considerable amount of money and Provost Fingland resigned his office as a result of all the criticism he got from the townsfolk.

Another great tale from about 160 years ago relates to a famous fight between the men of Sanquhar and a band of Irish navvies who were working on the Nithsdale section of the new Glasgow and South Western Railway. The work had attracted a lot of Irish labourers into the district. They frequently came into town and their presence was generally signalled by some uproarious goings on in the public houses of which Sanquhar had more than its fair share at the time.

Steeplechases were arranged to take place on the town common and a great gathering of people, including all of the navvies, to whom a holiday had been given, were present.

Horses belonging to the railway contractor, to the farmers and to the townspeople took part in the races. After one of the races, some of the Irishmen disputed the victory and following an angry exchange, one of them threatened to strike the jockey who had ridden the winner. A young lad of nineteen, who was standing by, warded off the blow and immediately became the object of the attack. A big navvy made a dash at him with a knife, which caught him upon the little finger of the right hand, making a nasty cut to the bone, the scar of which he bore all his days. In retaliation, the young lad felled the Irishman with his riding whip, and fighting his way out of the crowd, had to take to his heels with a host of howling navvies after him. He made tracks for the burgh as fast as he could, and leaping dykes and ditches, he soon outran his pursuers.

In the town he told what had happened and it was decided by the weavers, who formed the bulk of the Sanquhar population at the time that they should band themselves together and prevent the Irishmen from entering the town when the races were over. Armed with sticks and pokers, the weavers and other townsmen awaited the arrival of the Irishmen. They returned from the races down Helen's Wynd in a body and no doubt intended to make their way down the High Street. Instead they were met by the townsfolk standing shoulder to shoulder in closed ranks ready to repel them at the foot of the wynd. The Sanquhar men forced the Irishmen back past the Council House and out along the main road. Some rough hand-to-hand fighting took place and blows fell thick and fast that broke some bones. The Sanquhar men gained the day and effectively banished the Irishmen from the burgh.

Years later, one of the navvies, who had subsequently become a tramp, returned to Sanquhar to beg. He took great delight in going over the events of what he considered to be a "great day". He had been in many big rows and fights in Ireland, and claimed to be no novice in handling a shillelagh, but he said that never in all his experience had he encountered such antagonists as the Sanquhar weavers!

No chapter on equestrian related tales would be complete without relating that of Christopher Anderson's faithful and remarkable pony.

The family of Anderson has had a long and very interesting connection with Sanquhar and the Crawick Water, and in the first half of the nineteenth century was intimately associated with the coal mining industry. The family originally came from Lanarkshire where John Anderson was born in 1738. He spent his early years in Leadhills, where he married Margaret Dobie of a family long connected with the lead mining there. Somewhere about 1760 he settled in Sanquhar and was employed in the coal mines owned by Mr Barker and Mr McNab, and was at his death in 1780, in the employment of the latter.

Christopher Anderson, his son, was a remarkable man and was well-known in the district as the blind colliery manager. He had lost his sight at the age of twenty-one as the result of a dastardly assault by an opponent, who from behind the shelter of the corner of a house, struck him in the face with a thorn bush. Although thus early blinded he did not lose heart, but most courageously faced his misfortune. He got a job at the colliery and through the energy of his character, his natural ability, and the help of his devoted wife he rose rapidly and finally became manager and part owner of the business.

He succeeded so well that in 1816 he took the lease of Meikle Carco farm in Crawick Water, which he held until 1838 when he took the tenancy of Spango farm.

Early success nearly ended in ruin when his main partner in the collieries failed in 1841 leaving him burdened with debt. His two sons, John and Adam, would not allow him to declare himself bankrupt, but with the indomitable resolution and courage of their father, shared his liabilities and had the great satisfaction after their father's death of finally clearing off every shilling of his debts. The shock, however, was too great for the old man and brought on paralysis, of which he died three years later. There are some remarkable incidents of the blind colliery manager that are well authenticated and worth telling.

Part of blind Christopher Anderson's duties in the management of the Sanquhar collieries was to go around for orders and to collect accounts. When doing so he generally rode on a white pony, which knew the calls almost as well as the rider. When the pony was left outside a house, no persuasion by mischievous boys, or attempted force would make it move until his master came out.

On one occasion master and pony left Sanquhar after dark to go home to Meikle Carco. It had snowed heavily during the day and somewhere about the Orchard they stumbled into a deep drift. The pony struggled through to the other side, but the rider was forced off. When the pony realised there was no one on its back, it backed in its own tracks until Christopher was able to catch either the leather strap attached to the saddle, or the stirrup, and was then pulled by the pony to safety. He always declared the pony saved his life.

One morning, while Christopher was being assisted at the colliery by his full-grown but still unmarried son Adam, the latter was superintending the re-timbering of an "in-gaun-ee", or drift, that entered the braes from the Castle Holm. While engaged at this, the drift collapsed, and Adam was buried under a fall of earth. Great difficulty was experienced in rescuing

*"One of their wives was waiting
at the bridge with a lantern*

him on account of a timber having fallen across his loins, and it was feared that he could lose his life.

Word was sent to the blind father, asking him to come as quickly as possible. He happened to be near a pit-mouth some distance away. As travelling round by the road would take too long, the blind man insisted on being let down the pit. He then travelled as near as possible in a bee-line through the old workings that had not been travelled for years. He managed to reach his son just as he was being rescued after two hours of very strenuous exertion. Taking into account the constant changes in an old abandoned colliery, the feat of the old man was wonderful.

When Provost James Hamilton was the occupant of the Holm in Crawick he and the blind coal-master frequently visited each other. On one occasion the visit was by Christopher and went long on after dark. When he proposed going home, his friend naturally offered to see him safely across the bridge over Crawick Water. In those days the bridge consisted of three or four fir trees stretched across the river and tied together, but with no parapet whatever. There was no Holm "walks" then, but a path up the water side. After proceeding for some time, the blind man said, "Jeems, I rather think we're aff the road". The seeing man replied, "I hae been half thinking that mysel', but if we are aff't, I canna pit ye on't". So the blind man had to take his friend by the hand, and lead him to the bridge, where one of their wives, who had become alarmed, was waiting with a lantern.

Robert Burns

Chapter 10
Robert Burns in Upper Nithsdale

Upper Nithsdale has been the home to many famous writers and poets. James Hogg, the Ettrick shepherd was, for a while a tenant of Laight farm, on the banks of the Scaur in the parish of Penpont. He was never a successful farmer and used to try to negotiate the rent down to a level that he could afford. The Duke of Queensberry once asked him if he let him have the farm rent free would he make a profit. "Yes", replied James, "provided your Grace would stand between me and the rot and the February snow wreaths".

Undoubtedly the most famous Nithsdale resident was Scotland's bard, Robert Burns who was a tenant of Ellisland Farm for a while before becoming an exciseman. Indeed his duties in that respect regularly took him into the Nith and Cairn valleys. He had a particularly close circle of friends in Sanquhar that he met regularly in the Queensberry Arms, or Whigham's Inn as it was known locally. I have already documented his close association with Sanquhar in "Old Sanquhar Tales", so I will now relate some other stories of events that occurred in Thornhill and Wanlockhead.

Although Burns had his choice of good boot makers in Dumfries, he continued, from the time of his entering Ellisland until he died to get his boots from a Thornhill shoemaker. In fact, the last pair of boots that he wore – a pair of top ones – were made by Andrew Johnstone, who had a little shop at the foot of Old Street, where the Buccleuch Hotel now stands. For some reason he didn't get those boots within the promised time – they were three days late – prompting Johnstone to say "I was terrible feart he wad mak poetry about it".

A tale is told of how Burns attended a Thornhill fair in August 1790. In Old Street lived a poor woman, Kate Watson, who on these gala days ran an illegal drinking den. The poet entered the door and instead of immediately seizing the barrel that contained the contraband liquor the bard was in search of, he gave a nod, accompanied by a significant movement of the forefinger and brought Kate to the doorway. He then said, "Kate, are ye mad? Dinna you know that the supervisor and I will be in upon you in the course of forty minutes? Goodbye. Goodbye to ye

Townhead Street, Thornhill. These houses stood at the junction of Townhead and
New Streets. The middle house still stands today. The old lady's name is unknown.
Townhead Street was the site of the old village of Thornhill,
before the building of the new road, now Drumlanrig Street, in 1714.

at present". That friendly hint was not neglected. It saved a poor widow from a fine of several pounds.

There is another story connecting Burns in his capacity as exciseman with Thornhill. A woman called Jean Davidson, who kept a small public house, was suspected of putting more water in the whisky than was necessary or lawful. Burns accordingly called one day unexpectedly, and, of course, detected the irregularity at once. "Now, Jean, my woman", he said, putting his hand on the keg, "I canna tak this wi' me the night as it is owre late to go to Dumfries, but I'll seal it wi' the King's seal and lift it in the morning".

After he had gone to his lodgings for the night Jean sent for a local cooper. Acting on her instructions, he removed three hoops from the barrel, and underneath the third bored a hole. Through this hole Jean drew off about half of the diluted contents and poured into it an equal quantity of "well-set-up" whisky. The hole was plugged, the hoops replaced, and the condemned whisky was made into legal consistency without the King's seal being in any way impaired.

Next morning Burns called to lift the keg. "One meenit, Mr Burns", says Jean, "Ye micht just test that whisky to convince me, for I canna see hoo I've made sic a mistake". "Certainly, Jean", replied poor, unsuspecting Burns. "It means breaking the King's seal, but I can just mak anither".

The seal was broken, the sample drawn, tested, and miraculously was alright. Burns could not account for it. "Was there ocht wrang wi' me last nicht, did ye notice Jean?" he enquired. "Weel, Mr Burns, it's really no' for me to say, but – weel, I just thocht ye were fully smert wi' yer wee tester", she replied.

On one occasion Burns had gone to Wanlockhead in the course of his duties as exciseman, astride his faithful horse Pegasus. It was during the winter and Mennock road was slippery with ice. All who know that winding pass can well imagine the journey was one that had to be taken with great caution. Before he could return it was necessary for the safety of both the bard and his steed that the latter should have its shoes "frosted".

On calling upon the blacksmith of the village to get this necessary work done, he found him so busy with other work at the time that he was unable to attend to the wants of a stranger. By way of gaining the goodwill of the man of iron, Burns sat down in Ramage's Inn "at three o'clock" and penned the following;-

> With Pegasus upon a day
>   Apollo weary flying
> (Through frosty hills the journey lay)

On foot the way was plying.
Poor slip-shod, giddy Pegasus
   Was but a sorry walker;
To Vulcan then Apollo goes
   To get a frosty caulker.

Obliging Vulcan fell to work,
   Threw by his coat and bonnet,
And did Sol's business in a crack –
   Sol paid him in a sonnet.

Ye Vulcan's sons of Wanlockhead,
   Pity my sad disaster!
My Pegasus is poorly shod –
   I'll pay you like his master!

These verses were handed to Mr John Taylor, the resident manager of the mines, the employer of the smith, and a friend of Mr John Sloan, who had accompanied Burns on his laborious journey, and who, at the poet's request, added the following:- "J Sloan's best compliments to Mr Taylor, and it would be doing him and the Ayrshire Bard a particular favour if he would oblige them instanter with his agreeable company. The road has been so slippery that the riders and the brutes were equally in danger of getting some of their bones broken. For the poet, his life and limbs are of some consequence to the world; but for poor Sloan, it matters very little what may become of him. The whole of this is to ask the favour of getting the horses' shoes sharpened".

The verse and Sloan's note had the desired effect. The blacksmith, on learning who required his aid, at once left off the important work he had on hand and attended to the needs of Burns and his friend.

It scarcely requires to be added that the smith was well paid for his trouble. In later years it was his custom to boast that he had never been so well paid for work done as by Burns, who "paid him in siller, paid him in drink and paid him in verse".

John Taylor the mine manager belonged to no ordinary family. His father, Robert Taylor and his grandfather, John Taylor, after whom he was named, are buried in the graveyard of Leadhills. The tombstone there marking their resting place, was much sought after by visitors, for it bears a remarkable inscription, which is as follows:- "Sacred to the memory of Robert Taylor, who was during many years an overseer to the Scotch Mining Company at Leadhills and died May 6th, 1791, in the 67th year of

Highest home in Scotland, Wanlockhead, c1940

his age. He is buried by the side of his father, John Taylor, who died in this place at the remarkable age of 137 years".

There is some doubt as to the accuracy of that inscription and according to calculations by Rev. J Moir Porteous in his book, God's Treasure House of Scotland he was "only" 133 when he died. He seems to have been born in 1637, and as he died in 1770, Porteous points out he could only have lived for 133 years. That can be ascertained by a celebrated eclipse of the sun that took place in the year 1652, and the age at which young men were allowed to work underground.

Losing his father when just four years old, he washed ore when a boy for tuppence a day. For three or four years he had been a "kibble-boy" in the mine and was at the bottom of a pit called Winlock Shaft on the "dark Monday". One Thomas Millbank called down to him to tell the men below to come up and behold the wonder, for a curious cloud darkened the sun and the birds were falling to the earth. This was an event John Taylor frequently described.

John Taylor is undoubtedly Wanlockhead's most famous son. He had worked in lead mines in Durham and also worked in Argyle and Yorkshire before moving to Leadhills in 1733 when he was already 90 years of age and he went on to work for another 19 years as a labourer.

There is a story that when he was 100 he was put outside the door one night "in case God had forgotten him". Another tale is that, at 116, he went off on a fishing trip, got lost, stuck his fishing rod in the snow and walked back to a point from where he was rescued. When he had recovered, he went back, plucked his rod out of the snow and returned to begin his new lease of seventeen years of life.

John Taylor lived outside Leadhills at Gold Scars and was still walking the two miles into the village at the age of 128. A 19th century account of him at the Leadhills Reading Society – the oldest subscription library in Scotland, founded in 1741 says, "He was a thin spare man, about 5 feet 8 inches high, black-haired, ruddy faced and long visage. His breakfast was usually oatmeal porridge, for dinner meat and broth, and his chief drink malt liquor".

His teeth were good and firm till 1764 when he gave up chewing tobacco to save money and then lost the best of them in a few months. At length, with hardly any remains of bodily or mental faculties, this veteran of 133 years expired in the month of May 1770.

Chapter 11
The Roaring Game

The Sanquhar Curling Society, founded on 21 January 1774, is one of the oldest and can fairly claim to have the oldest records proving its existence. At the time of its formation, curling was a very popular game throughout the greater part of Scotland and was practised in almost every parish in the South Western counties. The game was originally thought to have been imported from the continent, probably from Holland or Germany. It appears likely that at first, curling was nothing other than a game of quoits practiced on ice.

It is speculated that the original game of quoits on ice was developed and sophisticated by the Scots and that Scotland is truly the birth place of curling, or the "roaring game" as it is called, due to the sound the stones make over the ice. The country at that time, although perhaps not now, possessed the very conditions of climate necessary to playing the game outdoors.

Life more than two centuries ago was of course very much different from our present circumstances and without the aid of television or radio, news was very much confined to local issues. It appears that the curling results in those days were eagerly anticipated. A story is told of a match between Sanquhar and a neighbouring parish where, before the shots had been counted up and an official result given, the general impression was that Sanquhar had been defeated. A party of Sanquhar curlers had settled themselves in the upper room of a public house and were engaged in comforting themselves over a "wee dram", when a messenger opened the door and announced the welcome news that Sanquhar was victorious by two shots. That announcement is said to have acted like magic on the entire company. Several curlers danced on the table, while others rushed to the stair head and, seizing a row of flower pots, threw them down the stairs.

Another story is told of a famous Sanquhar curler who left the loch in disgust after a severe defeat and, on making his way home, he met a number of townspeople who enquired how the game was going. He was so ashamed of the defeat that he would not admit to it and merely replied, "You'll see when you gang forrit". The curlers in those days took matters rather seriously!

Not only did the curlers themselves take defeat badly, but the townspeople thought that losing tarnished the good name of the parish. On one occasion, news of a crushing defeat for Sanquhar had been conveyed by telegraph to the town and when the curlers returned home, they were received with a storm of groans and hisses, and each skip had marked on his door the total number of shots that he had lost by.

The results of games were eagerly awaited in Sanquhar and a merchant, a Mr Halliday, offered a shilling to the first messenger to bring the news of a result. On one occasion, the messenger had to run a distance of twelve miles and collapsed in a state of exhaustion when he reached the town.

It should be remembered that two centuries ago there was little communication between towns, particularly in winter in country districts. Every little country town was isolated within itself and there was little social intercourse with neighbouring towns, so that curling matches between parishes were greatly looked forward to. The game was a common denominator as it was played by noblemen, clergymen, lairds, farmers, shopkeepers, tradesmen and labourers. They all met on common ground and on the ice the conventions of social life were set aside and the greatest freedom of intercourse allowed.

There was always a great deal of suspense and uncertainty regarding the games, as the state of the weather was crucial. The weather was watched anxiously and the sky eagerly scanned and every sign of a change was noted, duly weighed and discussed. It is said that some curlers would, on going to bed, hang a wet cloth out of the bedroom window and then rise periodically during the night to determine the keenness of the frost by the stiffness of the cloth.

The minute of the first meeting of the Sanquhar Curling Society reads as follows: - "On Friday the 21st day of January, 1774, near sixty curlers met upon Sanquhar Loch and had an agreeable game at curling. In the evening they dined together in the Duke of Queensberry's Arms in Sanquhar. After dinner, it was proposed that they should form themselves into a society under the name of Sanquhar Society of Curlers, and that a master should be chosen annually; which proposal was agreed to, and several other regulations respecting the constitution and order of the society were made. Accordingly, one of the oldest curlers being chosen President appointed a committee of the best qualified to examine all the rest concerning the Curler Word and Grip. Those who pretended to have these and were found defective were subjected to a fine, and those who made no pretensions were instructed. The Mr Alexander Bradfute in South Mains was chosen Master for the present year. The terms and prices of admission into the

Society were – submission and obedience to the Master, and discretion and civility to all the Members and Secresy. Fourpence sterling to be paid by everyone in the Parish and sixpence to be paid by anyone without the Parish as their admission; and liberty was granted to the Clerk and some other members to add whatever new members there were and to report those to the society at their next meeting".

Rules and regulations were mainly drawn up for the conduct of business of the society and did not cover the rules of the game itself. Article 5 of the rules of the society is particularly interesting. It reads, "The Masters are to give due warning to the players at all times when any game is to be played either among the rinks or with a different parish, and, in case of neglect, to be liable to pay the sum of one shilling; and any player, so warned, either refusing to come forward, or not giving a plausible reason for non-attendance, shall forfeit the sum of sixpence.

The Masters are to have the principal charge of their respective rinks, assisted by such of their own rinks as they shall appoint, not exceeding two, and every player is to submit, without murmur, complaint or reluctance to the Master's judgement of those nominated by him. The Masters are to use their endeavour to suppress swearing or abusive language on the ice among their players, and every person offending shall be fined of a sum not exceeding twopence".

It would appear that there was some Masonic-like secrecy about the membership of the society and that the Curler's Word was;-

> If you'd be a Curler keen,
> Stand right, look even,
> Sole well, shoot straight and sweep clean.

The Curler's grip seems to have been some sort of secret handshake. There were also different subtle and secret signals and handshakes between the skip and players indicating the type of shot that was to be played.

On admission to the society, each member was initiated with the password and the grip on the payment of the sum of fourpence, or sixpence according to whether he was a parishioner or not. In this connection, Wanlockhead was in the parish of Sanquhar and the club drew a lot of its strength from that village. The members of the club in Wanlockhead, because of the vow of secrecy, were unable to communicate the secrets of membership and so were unable to play with other curlers in Wanlockhead. In 1777 they presented a petition to the club asking for dispensation of the secrecy rules and this was granted so that they may join with other "Dodders" in the sport.

The usual practice when games were played against neighbouring parishes was to have two games of nine shots per player. One game was played for the dinner and the other was played for the drink, so that sometimes the dinner was won by one parish and the drink by the other. It is recorded that Sanquhar frequently had both the expense of their neighbours.

The practice of playing for dinner and drink prevailed until about 1830 when a motion was passed that at all parish spiels there should be no dinners, but that any member or rink may dine with the challenging party if they agreed to it. At the same meeting it was resolved that all parish matches be decided by shots. Previously they had been decided by the number of winning rinks, regardless of the aggregate shots gained or lost. The absence of the dinners was regretted by some as the cultivation and promotion of social intercourse and friendship was lost.

The first game Sanquhar played with a neighbouring parish was with Kirkconnel in January 1776, followed by one with Crawfordjohn later that month. These two were the only parishes played until 1784 when the first game with Morton, which is of course the parish name for Thornhill. Penpont was added in 1804, Durisdeer in 1830 and New Cumnock in about 1844. The matches with Crawfordjohn and Durisdeer ceased in about 1850 and thereafter Kirkconnel, Morton, Penpont and New Cumnock were the parishes with which the bulk of curling was played until the centenary of the Sanquhar club in 1874.

In 1867 the curlers of Nithsdale received a challenge from the Annandale curlers to play a game on Castle Loch, Lochmaben with one hundred and twenty rinks per side. It should be noted that the size of rinks had been reduced from the customary 8 men to 4 in 1853. Sanquhar parish was to provide 16 rinks – 8 from Sanquhar and 8 from Wanlockhead. The game was first arranged for Monday 21 January 1870, but there was a sudden and rapid thaw at 2am that morning. By common consent the game was called off and a special train that had been provided to convey the players to Lochmaben was allowed to return empty and the Wanlockhead curlers who had walked down from Wanlockhead had to walk home.

The game was, however, played later in the year on 31 December 1870 when Nithsdale won the game by 250 shots. Sanquhar distinguished itself by playing with great style and her 16 rinks were 103 shots up. The Sanquhar club considered that it had served Nithsdale with great distinction, as Wanlockhead were unable to supply their whole quota of rinks and Sanquhar had to send 14 rinks.

A good old row emerged out of this game. The facts were that Sir Sydney Waterlow had been elected Member of Parliament for the County of Dumfries in 1868. However, the election was declared invalid and at a re-election he was defeated. Despite that, he presented a silver cup to the curlers of the county. Nothing was heard of the cup until the Annandale v Nithsdale game, known as the "Dale" game.

After the game had been played, the curlers of Morton Parish claimed the cup on the ground that as a parish they had the rink contributing the most to the victory. A correspondence ensued in the Dumfries Courier. James Brown claimed the cup for Sanquhar on the basis that they had the highest average shots up per rink. The matter was resolved by the holder of the cup, Mr Clark, stating that the cup was not for play in the Dale game, but that Sanquhar had the best claim to the cup.

To understand the tension and suspense that a curling match generates, I quote the following tale about a Thornhill curler nicknamed "The Duke" and a match he played in at Thornhill from "Thornhill and its Worthies" by Joseph Laing Waugh; -

"Twenty – twenty; onybody's game". The Duke taps his box deliberately, takes a pinch of snuff, turns his body half round on his right heel, and takes up a position at the head of the tee. "Noo, George, my wee boy, ye see my cowe? Look steady at me, noo, like a man. Bonnily set doon, George; bonnily set doon! Min' that stane, noo boys. Bring him away a wee. Soop, I tell ye, soop. Canny! – Canny! Yes, a wee touch. Into the hoose wi' 'im boys – stop, I tell ye, stop – let him dee boys when he will. Graun', boys, graun'. Great's yer play, George, come up and look at it". As the stone lies within a foot of what the "Duke" calls the "tap o' the lily", a smile of satisfaction breaks over his countenance, and the snuff-mull is again brought into requisition.

Ay, the Duke was my hero on the ice, but let me sketch the outline of that picture which rises up before me out of the past, and shows clearly on the gliding slides of memory.

The wintry day is now at its close. The cheering shout, the wild huzzas lessen and lessen as rink after rink finish their score, and, jubilant or crestfallen, as the case may be, betake themselves to watch the final struggle of some others still in play.

The dying glow – rich, red, crimson-hued – of the wintry sun pierces the firs on the crest of the wood, shoots in lances of fire between their branchless trunks, and slant-wise, lies mirrored on the bosom of the icy board. Sounds, far away and euphonious, strike the ear – the distant bark of the shepherd's dog, the resonant ding-dong, ding-dong from the Auld Kirk tower, the rumble, low and intermittent, of the traffic on the station road. These blend and soften, linger for a moment, and then die away quietly and gradually on the far reaches of their echoes.

By degrees the concentration takes place. Gradually the crowd comes together. From four scattered groups they draw to three, from three to two, and then, on the semi-final dissolution, they congregate, where stands the Duke, on the head of the tee, and beside him a redoubtable opponent from the curling stronghold of Upper Nithsdale.

Ah, it is then the Duke is in his glory. The eyes of the whole curling community are turned upon him, and a tussle before him in which his heart delights.

Carefully is each pose studied; weighed, and well weighed, is every word; deliberate and emphatic is each decision. As stone after stone rests within the rings the situation becomes more complicated. To the eye of the amateur it is a tangled problem, but faith is pinned on the Duke. He knows each move and the value of each stone. The mull is often tapped, but its contents not so often "preed", for there are times when the snuff is within measurable distance of its receptacle, something takes place – some unlooked for turn in the game – and the pinch slowly percolates from between finger and thumb and scatters to the wind. So far, it is, as the Duke says, "onybody's game". But our old hero, on the ice, is always an optimist.

"If onything, its brichter for us", he says to the henchman, as that well-known worthy assumes the directorship. Then the Duke walks down to the stell. Half-way down the rink he halts and surveys the situation from that point. "Ah, it looks no sae bad", he mutters to himself, and half-skloyin', half-walking, as was his wont, he again moves stellwards.

As the Duke takes up his position the crowd is at its densest. "Gie me some licht, boys, staun' oot ahin", and the order is at once obeyed.

"Hoo much d'ye see o' that, Duke?" cries his henchman.

"Off an' on, about three inches".

"Weel, Duke, gie me that a yaird on and I'll gie ye the shot. Steady, noo, Jeems!"

The Duke stoops to conquer. It is the shot, above all others, on which he prides himself, and many anxious, excited faces are turned towards him. He is nerved to great endeavours, and feels he is the man of the hour.

With that sharp click which bespeaks a good delivery the stone leaves his hand. Straight as an arrow it makes for its target.

"Duke, ye're aff't! No: Yes! – No; I'm wranging ye; I'm wrangin' ye! Ye're richt, Duke; ye're richt – for ever richt!" And as the stone shaves the guard, and with a turn of the handle bears down on the exposed three inches of the shot, a shout escapes from the lusty lungs of the henchman.

But two can play at that game.

With that sharp click which bespeaks a good delivery the stone leaves his hand

His worthy opponent is no mean rival, and when the Duke again stands to position, it is to find a big Sanquhar stone exasperatingly near the tee, and almost dead guarded.

The henchman puts his cowe, handle down, brush up on the winner.

"Duke, gie me that, and dinna depend on the cowe. If ye get a "chirr' on this" – pointing to a stone lying at an angle of 45 degrees to the winner – "weel and guid, if ye slip, ye'll get the shot".

Such a craning of necks, such a long lane of white, excited faces. There was that silence, too which falls on a crowd when the balance is being struck; when on the dexterity of one man hangs the results of a keenly-competed match; when with bated breath, the final touch is given.

What a moment for the Duke! It was the fulfilment of a whole season's yearnings – the acme of satisfaction and the very delight of his heart. Never, even on a sweltering July day, did he pass the loch road-end, without casting longing glances toward Rashbriggs, and in his usual vocation his mind was oftener between the hogg and lines than on the marshy swamp he was draining. How often had he in these dreams imagined such a situation? Now was his wish fulfilled!

"Boys, will ye no' gie me licht?" he cries in a high-pitched, excited voice.

"Hearken to the request of his Grace", says the inimitable John Laing. The crowd gives way behind, and only the Duke's men remain within the rings.

A long, steady look, a moment of suppressed excitement, and then a tremendous outburst of huzzas, as the Duke's stone accomplishes its end. George McCubbin, the henchman, kicks with his heel the small of his back – a feat which only he can perform with grace – and flings his cap in the air. Tom McCaig hums "The Bonnie Lass o' Ballochmyle", and John Laing meets the Duke half-way down the rink, shakes him by the hand, and calls him the grand old man of Rashbriggs and the Provost of the Cuddy Lane.

*Curling on Morton Loch. The old name was the Whitemoss Loch
or sometimes the Kirk Loch or Rashbrig Loch.*

Buchan Ha'. This old house was named after Elspeth Mother Buchan who came from Irvine with her followers whom she had promised to take to Heaven.

Chapter 12
The Buchanites

The founder of this fanatical sect, known as "Luckie Buchan", with her religious assistant, the Rev. Hugh White, and the remainder of their following, when expelled from Irvine, found a resting place for a time at New Cample Farm, Closeburn,

This crafty, naturally clever woman was the daughter of John Simpson and Margaret Gordon, who kept a small wayside pub on the old road between Banff and Portsoy, at a place called Fortmacken, where she was born in 1738.

Her mother died when Elspeth, as she was called, was only three, and, her father having married again shortly afterwards, she was sent to live with strangers. They were so poor that the bed on which the girl slept consisted of a sack stuffed with straw placed on the floor and an empty sack for a covering.

At an early age she was employed as a cow-herd, but she was eventually taken into the service of a distant relative of her mother's who also taught her to read and sew. This lady married a native of Banffshire who owned estates in Jamaica, to which they set off, taking Elspeth with them. While waiting for a vessel at Greenock, she fell in with loose companions and parted company with her friends.

She next turned up at Ayr, where she took up with a potter called Robert Buchan, but to whom she was not legally married. Indeed, marriage in her estimation was unnecessary, a view which she afterwards repeatedly taught to her followers, in addition to her many fanatical doctrines.

It was said that Buchan was so ashamed of her loose moral conduct that he took her to Banff in the hope of improving her by a change of associates. Here he tried to establish an earthenware business, but failed. Subsequently he went to Glasgow and found employment in his trade, leaving Elspeth, a son, and two daughters at Banff. She then set up a small school for instruction in reading and sewing, though ill-qualified to teach either one or the other. Her conduct again, it was said, was unbecoming an instructor of youth and before long both school and family were neglected.

At this time (1774) she seems to have entered upon the fanatical career by which she afterwards became notorious, and which she maintained to the end of her life. Her behaviour rendered her offensive to the people among whom she lived, and their strong disapproval made it imperative that she left the district. She sought out her husband in Glasgow and rejoined him in March, 1781. Curious to say, it was said that he welcomed her back and for a time they lived together.

In December 1782 she met a Mr White, a minister from Irvine, for the first time. She had first heard him preaching in Glasgow as he assisted in a service and was captivated by his sermon and the flowery way he spoke. In a lengthy letter that she posted to him from Glasgow she made him acquainted with the fact in her characteristic manner. This was the start of an acquaintance between them that lasted until her death.

White proudly showed the letter to several of his flock, who were quite struck with the originality of the style and content. As a result she was invited to Irvine and became an inmate of the house. She had at this time entered into an extensive correspondence with clergy men in all parts of the country and seemed to have acquired a marvellous capacity for reciting whole chapters of Scripture.

For a time her new acquaintances were enamoured by her extraordinary gifts and deemed her quite an acquisition to their number.

Her time was wholly taken up visiting, solving doubt and expounding texts. By and bye, however, they began to look on her with less favour and finally a fair number called upon their minister to put her away as a dangerous person. This feeling grew, until eventually White was served with an indictment at the instance of several of his congregation. They set out the objectionable features in her creed and called upon him to say whether or not he accepted or repudiated them. Being thus taken to task, he at once acknowledged his adherence to her doctrines.

Meantime, seeing how matters stood, Mrs Buchan returned to Glasgow, but not without having the whole matter submitted to her. She gave her replies in letters beginning "My Dear Child", as she parentally addressed Mr White. In another letter she addresses the minister as "My Dearly Beloved Brother in Our Lord Jesus Christ". In this communication she "chides him in love" for not writing longer letters and not saying anything of "Bell" and the "dear child", referring to Mrs White and her infant.

The charge of heresy against White was to be tried by the Presbytery of Glasgow and Mrs Buchan was busily engaged in helping with the defence, as well as writing consolatory letters to Mrs White and to her husband, the accused

White's friends tried to dissuade him, in his own as well as in the interests of his wife and family, from pursuing such a suicidal line of conduct. They strongly advised him to renounce this frenzied, illiterate woman and return to soberness of thought and action, but to no avail. This is all the more unaccountable when White's reputed intellectual achievements are considered.

The Presbytery met in a meeting house in Glasgow which was crowded to excess during the trial. The unanimous finding was to depose White from the office of the ministry.

The closing of the doors of the church against him had the effect of making many more of both sexes join him, including a number of wealthy and influential people.

For a time White conducted services in his own garden and several times evil-disposed individuals took to throwing missiles amongst the congregation and otherwise disturbing the meetings. The feeling against the new sect increased until it assumed, at times, the proportions of a riot.

Many inexcusable outrages were perpetrated on its members, particularly on Mrs Buchan, who at White's request rejoined them at Irvine. No attempt on the part of the Magistrates seems to have been made to curb the violence of the community and brutal assaults were made, even to stripping Mrs Buchan naked and leaving her bruised and bleeding on one occasion.

The Magistrates of Irvine met in council on the morning of May Fair Day, 1784 and unanimously decreed that Mrs Buchan should be expelled from the burgh within the hour.

As soon as this decision was made known to the Buchanites, a meeting was hastily convened and held in White's house. The edict was only against the "Lady Mother", as they afterwards called her, but many of the people of Irvine belonging to her sect, as well as a small following from Perthshire, who were in Irvine at the time, decided to cast in their lot with her.

They started on their pilgrimage, each man with a staff in one hand and a small bundle in the other, and each woman in "kilted coats" and a small bundle tied to her waist. Mr and Mrs White were downcast, but Luckie Buchan was more than ordinarily cheerful, quoting apt passages of Scripture to fortify them in their trying hour.

The Magistrates came to see their order carried out. The company went forward, Mrs Buchan and Mr White leading and the rest, including children, following. The whole population turned out to witness the departure and assaults of a most inexcusable kind were committed on the poor, deluded company of folk.

The departure of such a well-dressed company, several of whom were people of substance, naturally excited every village through which they passed. "Our Lady", as they called Mrs Buchan, rode in front on a white pony, dressed in a scarlet cloak.

The first halt was at Dundonald, where they occupied a cart-shed and the open space in front of the fireplace in a kiln, as a result of a mistaken idea by the proprietor that their position was similar to that of the Covenanters, from whom he was descended.

At New Cumnock they had a hayloft. At Slunkford they weren't allowed a barn, or even the lee-side of a haystack, nor were they served much better at Edonhall. At Kirkconnel, which they reached on a Saturday evening, they got two good night's quarters with the use of a large room in a pub, where White preached on Sunday. He also preached at Thornhill.

The friends of one of the wealthy members of the band grieved at his folly and sought to detain him upon any and every pretence, until, as they said, "the glamour of the witch-wife was gone". For this purpose a warrant was issued and a posse of constables with messenger-at-arms were despatched to arrest and convey him back to Irvine. They overtook the Buchanites and executed their warrant, but allowed his wife and two children to proceed. Some others, afraid of a similar action, also returned to settle their affairs.

Deprived of their wealthy members, the society decided to call a halt at the first resting place they could find and await the return of their friends. This resting place they found at New Cample Farm, about a mile south of Thornhill.

Finding that the Irvine contingent didn't return as early as was expected, Mrs Buchan despatched letters to them. These she signed "Elspath Buchan", having previously in all her communications signed "Elspath Simpson".

The tenant of New Cample, a Mr Davidson, granted them the temporary use of a barn, but finding them ready customers for his various articles of produce for which they always paid on delivery, besides getting his farm work done, for which they would not make any charge, he was induced to allow them to remain longer than was at first arranged.

Their mode of living was quite basic – thoroughly communistic in principle – all things were held in common. They dined at one common table, in the most primitive fashion. Their beds, which consisted of heather bound up in bundles, about six feet long and four feet wide, were placed on the floor, with a narrow passage between. Each bed was for two people and their clothing served as pillows. Several of the wealthy members who had gone back to Irvine, including the one who had been arrested by the constables, returned and contentedly shared the common lot.

The relations of husband and wife were abandoned and the general opinion locally was that this communal life was purposely meant to conceal crimes of a shamefully wicked nature.

Mr Davidson intimated that he needed his barn to store the crops that he was about to harvest and proposed they should build a house, for which purpose he offered them ground. They gladly consented, and having all the necessary tradesmen among their company they set about constructing what the Closeburnians in derision named "Buchan Ha'", which name it bears to this day.

The house, a one-storey building, covered with heather, was thirty-six feet long and sixteen feet wide. It had a loft made with poles got from an adjoining plantation, and these were roofed with green turf. The most primitive bedsteads were constructed with sacks fitted with straw. The bed clothes consisted of a blanket below and one as a coverlet. There were only two beds downstairs in a closet adjoining the kitchen, while a trap-ladder led to the dormitory above. Two long tables, surrounded by stools, formed the furnishings, with the addition of a dresser, a meal chest and a few stools in the kitchen. In Mr White's closet there was a table and a few chairs intended for visitors.

People came from far and near to see Luckie Buchan and her following. At first White preached almost daily to large assemblies, that included the clergymen of the surrounding country. Mrs Buchan usually wound up the services in her own special vein. By and bye the gatherings diminished and the denunciations of the pulpits were said to inflame the minds of the people against this unconventional community until they resolved to expel them from the parish.

The 24th December, 1784, a night when there was no moonlight and about a foot of snow on the ground, was appointed for the expulsion. Lights were seen on the surrounding hills and as signals for muster, guns were fired. In a short time a number of men, estimated to be at least one hundred strong, approached. They were armed with bludgeons, pitchforks and flails.

As they drew near, the Buchanites went inside and fastened the door and all the windows. When the house was surrounded, one man rapped and demanded admission. No answer was given so the rap was repeated more violently, accompanied with a threat that if Luckie Buchan and the man-child White were not instantly turned out of the house they would reduce it and its inmates to ashes. Another attempt was made and finally, with the aid of large stones, the door and windows were all smashed. The invaders rushed into the house and were apparently surprised to find the inmates all quietly seated there.

An inspection of the company was made, to find Friends Mother and White, and on failing, they demanded to know where they were. On being informed that they were beyond their reach, the whole house was searched. Finding themselves foiled, the marauders bundled the poor, deluded creatures out to the rigours of a winter night, with a foot of snow lying, and then wreaked their vengeance upon the articles of furniture. Eventually their fury abated and the Buchanites were allowed to return from the Thornhill road, to which they had been dragged and driven, to find Buchan Ha' sacked and almost in ruins.

The inmates of Buchan Ha' were not wholly unaware of what was in store for them. The kind-hearted factor at Closeburn Castle, learning what was likely to happen, invited Friends Mother and White to the castle until the assault was over, and thus they escaped the fury of this ill-advised mob.

The miscreants did not, however, as in the case of the Irvine rioters, escape the fangs of the law. Upwards of twenty of them were fined by the sheriff for the offence.

A charge of blasphemy against White and Buchan was lodged with the ecclesiastical authorities in Dumfriesshire after the riot, but nothing came of it.

The Buchanites did not make many converts in Closeburn and even started to lose disenchanted members.

Mr White published several works, amongst which his Divine Dictionary ranks as the principal. This production was said to be a rare example of knowledge and ignorance, reason and fanatical zeal, embodied in one person.

According to the expressed statements of the two principals in this peculiar sect, the time was nigh at hand when the abode in the wilderness was to cease and the translation to heaven to take place. The wonderful woman of the Apocalypse, whom Mrs Buchan claimed to be, and who was "seen in heaven after having brought forth a man-child", was to remain in the wilderness one thousand two hundred and three score days. She dated her time in the wilderness from the conversion of White and her first visit to Irvine, he being "the man-child that was to rule all nations with a rod of iron". They kept singing one of White's so-called hymns, the refrain of which was:

"O! Hasten translation, and come resurrection!

O! Hasten the coming of Christ in the air".

As a preparation for the translation they entered upon a period of fasting that threatened to end in death by starvation to some who kept it too rigidly.

At long last the glorious day arrived on which they were all to be taken up to heaven. Platforms were erected for them to wait on till the wonderful hour arrived, Mrs Buchan's platform being exalted above all the others. The hair of each head was cut short, all but a tuft on the top for the angels to catch them by when drawing them up.

So full was White of the idea of being carried aloft without tasting death that he dressed himself in his canonicals, put on his gloves, and walked about scanning the heavens. Crowds of country people were looking on and expecting every minute that the sound of the Archangel's trumpet would break upon their ears.

The momentous hour came – every station for ascension was occupied – thus they expected any moment to be wafted into the land of bliss. A gust of wind came, but instead of wafting them upwards it capsized Mrs Buchan's platform. After this unexpected downfall, her word didn't carry so much weight with her followers.

The failure and exposure in the sight of so many was humiliating in the utmost degree to Mrs Buchan, and White was decidedly changed in his manner towards her after the occurrence. The disappointment seems to have been too much even for him.

The debacle led to the wealthier members of the sect becoming disillusioned and they abandoned it. White was summoned to attend a court of the county magistrates at Brownhill on January 1787 to give proof that none of the society would become a burden on the parish. The wealthy portion having forsaken them, he could not give the necessary guarantee, so he, together with the rest, were ordered to depart from Dumfriesshire by the tenth of the following March.

This was "driving them into the wilderness again". They didn't know where to run, but through the intervention of Mr Davidson, they obtained a lease of Auchengibbert, a wild moor-land farm in the parish of Urr in the Stewartry of Kirkcudbright, then owned by Mr John Bushby, Sheriff-Clerk of Dumfriesshire. Admittance could not be obtained until the Whitsun term, but the old mansion of Tarbreck, near Kirkpatrick Durham, was procured as a temporary abode.

The date on which they had to set out duly arrived, and to escape a scene such as they experienced at Irvine they moved off at one o'clock in the morning of 10th March, 1787.

The depleted band continued to hold meetings, which were at first well attended, but finally the numbers declined and they made no converts

Brownhall Inn. This famous old coaching inn stands about ¾ mile south of Closeburn village on the main road. Robert Burns was a frequent visitor when on his excise duties. The landlord at the time, one Mr Bacon, retained an interest in the poet. After Burns' brother Gilbert became tenant of Dinning Farm near Closeburn in 1798, and then sold the contents of the house two years later, the bed in which the poet was born was purchased by Mr Bacon. His groom, Joe Langhorne, slept in the bed for many years and eventually bought it himself in 1829, moving thereafter to Dumfries, where a relative is supposed to have cut it up and made it into snuff-boxes. By the date of this photograph the inn had reverted to a farmhouse, which it still is.

in Galloway. In a short time the same outcry against their conduct and views on the part of the people of the Stewartry was heard, as it had been everywhere else.

White was now more concerned to see others well employed than to work himself, and he was also accused of paying more attention to his wife and children and gathering gear, than on the general interests of the common good. He spent most of his time accusing the Lady Mother of deception and fraud.

Meantime Luckie Buchan sickened and gave indications of her end drawing near, and, in spite of all her prophecies to the contrary, she expired on the morning of 29th March, 1791. Before speech left her she assured all the bystanders that she was the third person in the Godhead and could not die. Though she might appear to be dead she only slept and in six days would return to life.

A rude coffin was prepared and the body placed in it and concealed in the barn, while the death was kept a secret from the outside world. The faithful maintained that a sweet perfume exuded from the body and filled the room.

At the end of the six days, when there had been no appearance of returning life, the body of Mrs Buchan was secretly buried by White during the night in Kirkgunzeon Kirk-yard. A recently made grave was opened, the newly-interred coffin lifted, and that of Mrs Buchan placed in its stead. The disturbed coffin was then laid on top of Mrs Buchan's and the grave closed up again.

Three weeks after the death a demand was made by the Sheriff, Sir Alexander Gordon, for proof of the interment to satisfy public feeling, which was very strong on the point. White met him at midnight at Kirkgunzeon Kirk-yard, when the bodies were again exhumed. After the Sheriff was satisfied a re-interment was performed and the grave closed.

White and about thirty of the party left Auchengibbert on 11th June, 1792 and shortly afterwards sailed for America. Mrs White died of fever about a year after her arrival in America and her husband found employment as a schoolmaster in the State of Virginia. He occasionally varied his occupation by preaching, but he was never known to refer to his former life, or allude to his former whimsical doctrines.

There still remained a small remnant in Galloway, about fourteen in all, of whom three were old women. They left the farmhouse of Auchengibbert, and built a cabin on the former tenant's sheep pens, and enclosed a piece of moor-land for a garden. The women took up spinning, while another member of the party, Duncan Robertson, turned to wheel making. They were credited with introducing the two-handed spinning wheel into

Galloway. Some of their women had the reputation of curing diseases and distempers which baffled the most skilful physicians. They were industrious in their habits and prospered.

All their farm utensils, barn and stable doors, corn sacks and carts were marked in large characters, "Mercy's property". In time their carts were marked "The people of Larghill", and finally, "George Kidd, farmer, Larghill", this being the name they gave to their new house.

On the opening of the present road between Dumfries and Castle Douglas, in 1800, the Buchanites purchased five acres of ground for houses and gardens at Crocketford. On one of the lots they built the first house, which in later years became the inn of the village. Altogether they spent about £900 on land and buildings, and in fact the village was founded by them. It was here that they established a graveyard, Mrs Gibson being the first to be interred in it, and the last Mr Andrew Innes. Alongside Innes, and in the same grave, was placed the remains of Mrs Buchan, which Innes had again resurrected and kept for some years in the coffin in a small lean-to which he built attached to his house. His last instructions were regarding this matter of burial, and the villagers and as many from the surrounding district crowded to witness a spectacle unique of its kind.

With this ceremony ended the career of a sect whose pretensions and absurdities were unique in Scotland.

One of the early followers to abandon the movement, Mr Hunter, who had been the town clerk of Irvine, was involved in a bizarre and humorous conversation concerning the mortality of Mrs Buchan.

Soon after her death, and before any account of it had reached the town of Irvine, Hunter met a horse dealer who had just returned from Dumfries Fair. Addressing the dealer he asked: "What news from the south country, John?" "None that I remember", replied the man of horses, "Except that your old friend, Luckie Buchan's deid at last". "Oh! No! John", replied Hunter, "that is no' the case and never will be in this world!" "Weel", said John hastily, "If she's no' deid her frien's in Galloway ha'e played her a devilish trick, for they ha'e buried her".

What they said about Rog's last book,
Old Sanquhar Tales:

"A fascinating collection of folklore passed down the generations" – Sunday Post

"The mystical and intriguing world of folklore is aptly combined with historical facts" – The Scots Magazine

"Tales to scare your granny with" – The Scottish Farmer

"A fascinating glimpse into the past" – The Dumfries and Galloway Standard

"Both fascinating and light-hearted – an easy read" – The Nithsdale News

ISBN 978-1-907931-03-1

£9.99

9 781907 931031 >